A
Fenland
Christmas

Compiled by Chris Carling

ALAN SUTTON

First published in the United Kingdom in 1990 by
Alan Sutton Publishing Limited · Phoenix Mill ·
Far Thrupp · Stroud · Gloucestershire

First published in the United States of America in 1991 by
Alan Sutton Publishing Inc · Wolfeboro Falls ·
NH 03896–0848

Reprinted 1995

British Library Cataloguing in Publication Data
Carling, Christine 1946–
A Fenland Christmas.
1. East Anglia. Fens. Christmas, history
I. Title
394.26828209426

ISBN 0–86299–749–6

Library of Congress Cataloging in Publication Data
applied for

Typeset in Garamond 12/13.
Typesetting and origination by
Alan Sutton Publishing Limited.
Printed in Great Britain by
The Guernsey Press Co Ltd.

Hetty Pegler's Christmas

CELIA DALE

Once the Fens were a world apart, a land of water and peaty bogs dotted with islands. A misty and mysterious land peopled by fishermen, fowlers and reed-cutters who walked on stilts when the waters rose. Even after the Fens were drained, the region remained apart – a flat, peat-black landscape, criss-crossed by dykes and embankments, with scattered villages and isolated cottages, just like Hetty Pegler's in Celia Dale's ghostly Christmas tale.

The small flint cottage on the edge of the Fens was mellow with the light of innumerable rush dips. From the open windows came the heart-warming scent of roasting meat. The windows had to be open in spite of the choking mist that crept damply in, so that Hetty Pegler would know when her guests were arriving.

Along one wall of the living-room was a trestle table with mugs and tankards; some of earthenware or crude glass, and others of pewter. Old Hetty hobbled round leaning on a stick, her bright black eyes taking in all the details to see her friends would be comfortable.

Drawing her shawl close around her shoulders she looked at the white scrubbed table in the middle of the room. Yes, it

· A Fenland Christmas ·

A world apart – the River Ouse, near Earith

would do. Pewter plates for the favoured; wooden platters for the rest.

Sniffing appreciatively she went towards the back kitchen which was divided from the other room so that Hetty could entertain certain special and private friends away from the prying eyes of her two serving girls, who were now preparing the Christmas meal.

'You're doing well,' she said to Tamsin and Armine, the buxom girls perspiring and striving over the spit and lifting lids from the heavy saucepans on the fire. Tamsin wiped her forehead with the corner of her apron.

'Plenty of mulled ale, mind,' warned Hetty, going forward and putting on the crisp fat of the meat a finger which she

licked. 'Lovely,' she said, closing her eyes, 'That'll suit ol' Mo' to a T. Open the window wider, gals,' although she knew the rush lights would flicker in the draught.

'It'll cool it all down, ma'am,' said Armine.

'Ne'er mind. No matter,' replied Hetty, her cheeks red from the fire and the agitation of old age. 'I want to hear when they all come. There must be a Christmas welcome for 'em.'

'What hour d'you reckon it is?' asked Armine of Tamsin, who peered closely at the new-fangled clock on the wall.

'As I can see, it's near ten of the clock. Time for 'em to start comin'.'

'Aye-aye,' sighed Hetty, limping away. She opened wide the front door, which groaned and complained on its hinges. The soft wreathing mist came in like an eager guest. As she stood in the damp silence there came the calls of marsh birds talking in their sleep.

She became aware of the liquid sound of a boat on the water. Presently the shipping of oars made her even more alert. With a great deal of grunting and swearing a male figure emerged. She could hear his heavy boots squelching in the mud. As he stumbled towards the light she called out. 'Come you in, me old tiger. It's bin a long time.'

'How are ye, me flower,' he answered. He held out his arms and in their brief embrace he seemed taller and younger and in his eyes she resembled one of the delicate flowers of the Fen.

They went into the cottage and he sat in a stout wooden chair by the fire. Hardly had he begun to drink the spicy ale put into his hand by Armine, than the sound of another boat was heard. Again the shipping of oars. A giant of a man appeared in the doorway, kicking off his boots and smoothing the damp from his hair with a huge hand. Hetty went to greet him.

'Sam, me old love, come in. There's mulled ale by the gallon to warm you.' A cavernous grin showed above his beard.

Then Mo' sitting by the fire got to his feet and with a great show turned back his sleeves.

'Now then,' he growled. Sam took a defensive stance. Tempers were high.

'Now then, let each other be. It's all gone and finished this many a year,' persuaded Hetty and she signed to Armine to bring a brimming measure of ale for Sam. Shamefacedly both men sank into chairs and stared at their feet.

Then small pattering steps sounded on the cobbles outside. Shrill laughter and a shy tap on the door. With a glory in her face Hetty let in two little girls of about six years old, who, a little hampered by their long skirts, almost tripped over the threshold into her arms.

Kneeling down Hetty hugged them to her. 'Me loves. Me doves. How've you bin?'

'All right, mother. The time goes so quick.'

'A posset for the babes,' she called. 'A milk posset. No ale for them.'

Happy and laughing, they sat on low stools in the inglenook and played with the cats dozing in the warmth. Mo' put out a hand to fondle the children's bright curls. Tamsin looked in, tousled and flushed. 'Roast's done, ma'am, and the pudding likely to boil dry.'

'There's just two we're waiting on, gal. They won't be long. Get on with the serving. They'll not be late.'

Someone was coming, singing a little hoarsely. Nearer and nearer came the song until it stopped outside the door. Hetty opened it to a tall, wild-looking young woman with tousled hair and frightened eyes. 'Come in, Pernel. We were waitin' on you.'

The newcomer stepped into the misty hot fug of the room. 'Is this all?' asked Mo'. 'For if it is, shet that door.'

'Yes, all but,' soothed Hetty, going to fetch a hot drink for Pernel, who smiled after sipping, and said it was comforting

Holm Lode, a lonely spot in the heart of the Fens

to her poor throat which still hurt after all that time. 'Ne'er mind,' whispered Hetty. 'S'all over these dunnamany years.'

'I got a hunger on me heavier nor a guv'ment man's staff,' grumbled Sam. 'Don' we have no vittles?'

Hetty went to the door and listened. The marsh birds murmured in their dreams again and that was all. 'Reckon he ain't comin',' she said sadly, turning back into the room. Gathering mugs and tankards she went into the kitchen, where, with all the activity going on, there was scarcely room for her to refill the drinking vessels for her guests. 'Get on, Mo' and you, Sam, and put chairs up to the table and set you down,' she called.

It took her some time to carry in the heavy mugs and tankards one by one, while Tamsin brought in the plates.

· A Fenland Christmas ·

Hetty smiled at the two little girls who sat with their noses at table level as there were no cushions. When all was served a small plate was brought, full of meat for the cats and a tinier one for the tame rats who scurried from under a large oak chest.

'E'n't Alice a going to come? I'd a thought she'd a come with you,' Hetty said to Pernel.

'She tried, but they kept dragging her back. But she'll get here somehow.'

One of the children looked up with a scream. A white object was bobbing at the window. Had the moon fallen from the skies? Hetty followed the children's gaze, then screeched back her chair on the scrubbed flag floor and went with lame speed to the door. It was Alice who came in amid scarves of mist. 'Good evenin' to you all,' she said, her hands to her throat, which was badly bruised.

'How are ye?' asked Sam, sopping up gravy with a hunk of bread. 'It's all of a year since we met.'

'Seems longer than that,' answered Alice, 'what with me neck always paining.'

Pernel looked up. 'You still complainin'? Mine's nearly as bad and I'm not always croakin'.'

'You went quicker,' Alice reminded her.

'Best meal I've had for a year,' said Mo', loosening his belt.

'Me too,' added Sam, massaging his paunch.

'Best meal for a year. That's good,' and Hetty laughed shrilly.

As Armine and Tamsin cleared away she reminded them to save the scraps for you-know-who.

'Who's that?' piped up one of the children.

'I told you last Christmas we mustn't say 'is name. It might bring evil on us so you couldn't come next year.' As a diversion the second little girl said she felt sick. Hetty gave a tender smile. 'Your eyes always were bigger nor your belly,' she said. 'Go sit in the chimney corner and play with the cats.'

6

· *A Fenland Christmas* ·

Wicken sedge fen, Christmas, 1971

It was not until the pudding was being enjoyed that a scratching and whining was heard at the door. Heavy thuds came on the stout wood. When Hetty opened the door there stood a large black dog, almost as big as a donkey. The cats jumped onto high shelves and the rats scrambled under the safety of the chest. The dog came in and Armine rushed to bring in a large dish of scraps. The huge dog assuaged its hunger.

Hetty went to look at the clock. Midnight was not far off. She told Tamsin they'd all have one last sup of ale, and settled herself in a chair between Pernel and Alice. The large black dog sat with its chin on her knee.

A silence so deep had fallen on the little group that they started when the clock wheezed and the weights slowly fell as it struck twelve. 'Well, me dears. It's come,' Hetty said. Then getting up she straightened herself proudly, holding on to the back of Mo's chair.

· A Fenland Christmas ·

All raised their heads to listen as she intoned:

> Alive or dead
> You've all been fed.
> Do not grieve,
> But take your leave.

Sam and Mo' were the first to get up. 'Goodbye, me beauties,' said Hetty, kissing them. 'I always loved you both.' They bade farewell to the rest, before going out into the mist. A few seconds later there came loud quarrelling voices and the sounds of fists on flesh. There were cries as the men fell into the water. Arms threshed, legs flailed, as the two of them gurgled to their death for the love of Hetty.

The next to go were Pernel and Alice. ''Til next Christmas,' they said as they left the cottage, their feet slipping on the wet cobbles. Hetty listened expectantly. Then it came. The screams of the women, protestations of innocence and last of all strangled curses before the final gasps.

She turned back into the warm, food scented room and gazed at the two little girls lying in each other's arms in the inglenook, their faces pale, eyes closed. Just as they had lain all those years ago when she had unwittingly killed them by an overdose of opium when they had ague. She leaned over them. 'My pretties,' she said softly. 'You'd a bin women grown by now with babes of your own.' And even as she looked at their soft innocence they became misty wraiths and disappeared.

'Ah ha,' sighed Hetty, sinking into a chair, and the great dog went to her, putting a sympathetic paw on to her lap. She thought of the friends who spent two hours of each Christmas with her. ''Twas a pity,' she mused, thinking of Alice and Pernel who were hanged as witches when they were young.

It was fortunate that Hetty herself, an even more skilful witch, had remained undetected, for by her incantations and

the burning of herbs she was able once a year to bring her friends together again. The only condition being that when they left after the Yule-tide feast they did so in the manner in which they died. Sighing, she patted the dog's head. At least she always had Black Shuck for company.

Christmas Memories

MABEL DEMAINE

Though towns such as Cambridge, Wisbech and King's Lynn have prospered well enough, Fenland village life has traditionally been hard. Even at Christmas pleasures for most people were simple. Born in 1908, Mabel Demaine was brought up in the fen village of Haddenham. In Reflections of a Country Woman, *a collection of her reminiscences, she recalls the Christmas of her childhood.*

Peeping through the curtains to see the village bandsmen clustered around a lighted lamp tied to a pole, hearing 'Hark the Herald' and 'O come, all ye faithful' played with great gusto, joining with other young people as soon as darkness fell to tour the village singing these same well-loved Christmas hymns – these are my earliest recollections. Deep snow and

9

Haddenham's bandsmen, who, as Mabel Demaine recalls, used
to go round the village at Christmas playing carols 'with great
gusto'. Pictured around the turn of the century

sparkling frost added to the pleasure — why did we never feel
the cold in those days?

There were no luxuries. Home-made paper chains and holly
decorated our rooms and a pile of logs filled our hearth.
Home-made cakes and puddings and mincemeat filled the
pantry shelves. A box of dates, a dish of nuts, oranges and
apples and a bottle of ginger wine — this was our Christmas
fare.

Christmas Eve was always a busy time for my mother,
stuffing the goose, preparing the vegetables, getting the
children off to bed early — this was no trouble on Christmas
Eve, the night when Father Christmas came. I can remember
trying to keep awake, waiting to see him arrive, at the same
time being somewhat fearful of some stranger filling that long

A snowy winter in the village of Wicken in the 1920s

stocking of my father's which hung at the foot of my bed.

I can still recall the rustling sound that stocking made when I awoke next morning and pushed my feet down the bed towards its bulging sides – an orange in the toe, a few nuts and sweets, a handkerchief – just a few simple things were all it contained – and yet what a joy and thrill they gave me.

My younger brother and I used to have our Christmas Day tea with some elderly relatives who lived two miles away. I wish I could make a ground rice cake like the one we had for tea – no rich Christmas cake could compare with that rice cake with its sugary, buttery, mouth-watering taste – how I would have liked a second slice!

After tea we played dominoes and draughts and I spy and then ate hot mincepies with a cup of cocoa. Muffled up with scarves and coats we walked home.

I can well remember those walks over fifty years ago. It was always moonlight and frosty, and how the frost did sparkle – and the stars – I watched the stars, they were so bright, and a shooting star gave me a shiver down my spine. It seemed such a fearful and frightening thing. I never see a shooting star now without being reminded of those walks home on Christmas nights.

Looking back on those bygone Christmases, why did I enjoy a walk in frost and snow then, and now I hate to even step out of the door or leave the fireside for a short while? Does the cold get colder as we get older, or do our likes and dislikes change? We roasted chestnuts and almost roasted ourselves by our open fires and then hugging a hot brick wrapped in flannel we went to bed contented with simple pleasures, finding time to think of the real message of Christmas, of peace on earth and good will to all men.

Old Christmas

How far do we have to go back to find a really idyllic Christmas, snow on the ground, Yule log crackling, wassail bowl steaming, young and old full of festive cheer? The Victorian era is not far enough if this poem, published in 1889 in the Wisbech Standard, *is anything to go by. A hundred years ago, it seems, the Victorians too were looking back. Then as much as now the golden age of Christmas belonged to a distant past.*

· A Fenland Christmas ·

Old Christmas is a 'wight' of worth; a 'rhyte goode' hearted
fellow,
Full of quaint sports, of playful pranks, and feelings ripe and
mellow,
For when the days are dark and dim, and all things dull and
drear,
He cometh like some faithful friend to bring us happy cheer.

He looketh hale in his green age, hath sunshine in his smile,
With rosy dimples in his cheeks; and heart devoid of guile,
His merry wrinkles twinkling out, all hearts are sure to win,
And young and old rush to the door, and joy to let him in.

With holy boughs and berries red, he gladdeneth our eyes,
And gladdeneth our stomachs too; with puddings and mince
pies,
With 'Baron Beef' and brave 'Sir-Loin', with turkey, goose and
chine,
With good old ale, old customs too; old friendships and old
wine.

And now he sits him down in state; within his old armchair,
While children, and grandchildren all, will cluster round him
there,
He piles the huge 'Yule' log on high and makes a blazing fire,
And cries good cheer and welcome all, like an old English
Squire.

He playeth with the children too, and joineth blind man's buff,
And rompeth like a boy again, and getteth many a cuff.
Before the crackling log he sits, and roasts the chestnuts
brown;
And scrambles up the 'snap-dragons'; and sups the 'lambs
wool' down

13

· *A Fenland Christmas* ·

He mindeth not a peppering of snowballs in the cold;
Nor yet a bump upon the ice, although he may be old;
And tho' Jack Frost in spiteful sport, may take him by the
nose,
He still laughs right good-humouredly at pinchings, bumps
and blows.

And he can sing a good old song of battle axe and lance,
And tell a good old story too, can foot a good old dance,
And while around in merry mood the 'wassail bowl' doth go,
He never fails to kiss the girls beneath the mistletoe.

Sometimes he buttons up his coat; and when the snow lies
high,
And wintry winds blow savagely from out a stormy sky,
He takes his walks of charity, and goes from door to door,
And good old Christian as he is remembereth the poor.

For Oh, he never can forget, in all his gayest mirth,
The Lord who brought goodwill to man and gave him peace on
earth,
And while the gladsome song of joy, his cheerful heart doth
raise,
With gratitude for blessings pass'd, he giveth God the praise.

Then joy to merry Christmas, and many may we spend,
Surrounded still by kith and kin, by neighbour and by friend;
Let's sing a song of faith and hope, nor thanklessly repine,
While One above can turn in love, life's waters into wine.

Memories of a Soham Butcher

KEN ISAACSON

The run-up to Christmas is a busy time for shopkeepers, and none more so than butchers. Ken Isaacson was a butcher in the Fen village of Soham, as was his father before him. In his recently-published memoirs, Life in the Meat Trade, *he takes us behind the scenes of the butchery business at Christmas. In the 1920s and 1930s the festive season started with a trip from Soham to London for the Smithfield Fat Stock Show.*

Every year at Christmas from about 1922 father used to go up to London to the Smithfield Fat Stock Show, then held in the old Islington Hall, to buy fat cattle for his Christmas trade.

When I say fat cattle I really mean fat cattle. They used to weigh about seventeen to eighteen hundredweight and had backs as wide as old-fashioned kitchen tables. You would need a fantastic dripping trade to deal with all that fat now.

Father would do his day's work, then catch a train in the evening and go up to London for the sale which did not start until ten o' clock at night. Then he would return home on the milk train, as it was then called, and be back in time to have a shave and wash, a good breakfast, and open the shop. They sure bred them tough in those days!

15

· A Fenland Christmas ·

One day, when I was about knee-high to a grasshopper, my father took my brother and I to Islington Hall to let us have a look at all those beautiful fat animals he had told us about.

This most wonderful event of our lives took place about the middle of the week. The show always started on a Monday — that was the night of the sale of the fat beasts, so father had already been along and purchased his animals. Mother had to stay at home and run the business while we were away and there was no one more competent than the 'Missus' as she had always been called, to do the job.

It was our first trip to London but I don't remember much about the journey except being told, 'When we get there, don't you go wandering off. Keep hold of my hand because there's a lot of sharks in London.' My God, I was petrified! It was years later I found out what he meant.

Arriving at Liverpool Street our first call was 'Dirty Dick's' to get the 'Missus' a bottle of port, a sort of compensation for staying at home. Then on to the show — and what a show! My brother and I were amazed to see the cattle, all the different breeds, just simply tons of rolling blubber. And after that the sheep and lambs, with flat backs, and dyed yellow, and some black; then the great big fat pigs, some with long noses, some with snub noses, black ones, white ones, brown ones, spotted ones. We were having a truly marvellous day.

'Look, Eric, there's the bullocks Dad bought.'

'Where's the others, Dad?'

'They're better than old Ted Leonard's, ain't they, Dad?'

At the end of the day two tired but happy little boys slept most of the journey home in the train and father almost had to carry us from the station.

Christmas joints on display

On the Saturday morning after the Smithfield Show the cattle Dad had purchased would arrive on Soham station. I can

A Christmas display of meat – Ted Leonard outside his
butcher's shop in Soham High Street in pre First World War
days

remember helping to lead these great rolling hulks of blubber
through the streets on halters. The walk from the station was
about all they could manage and they had to be rested all
afternoon in their stalls ready for the evening show.

In their pens the prize bullocks were brushed, combed,
sprayed with water and their coats curled and parted right
down the middle of their backs. Then ribbons were put around
their great necks and rosettes stitched to their new halters, and
when all was ready these magnificent animals were led out by
the light of father's flare lamp, and lined up facing the shop.
Father would stand at the shop door, as proud as could be,
with his long blue serge smock, as thick as an overcoat, white
apron and a hard, starched collar – the real, old fashioned
butcher craftsman.

This was one of the highlights of the year, as everyone used
to turn out on the night to see his Christmas joint on the hoof.
The orders would be booked that night by father and mother

· A Fenland Christmas ·

Ted Leonard's great-grandson, Tim, with a Highland bullock
brought back to the family butcher's shop from the Smithfield
show in the 1950s

while my brother and I and the apprentice boy hung on to the
halters of the bullocks. In those days on a Saturday night not
one car would pass to upset the animals. Now and again a
horse and cart would go by and make the bullocks snort, but it
was mostly the cart lanterns that unnerved them.

All evening long big fat farming types would walk around
these bullocks, admiring them and saying something like,
'Cut my joint off this one, Ernie,' 'About eighteen to twenty
pounds of rib and a stone of fat off this one, Ernie,' 'Can I have
a good hod off this heifer, Ernie,' 'Put me a couple of stone of
this one in brine for the New Year, Ernie.'

These were the proportions of the joints for Christmas then,
and when the orders were cut they were something to see. Ribs
of beef were cut in twos and right through – by this I mean the
eye of the rib, the middle and the brisket, this was rolled right

round, skewered and tied – and it was as big round as a dartboard with about three inches of sheer fat on the outside.

But here I am with the orders cut and the bullocks not yet slaughtered. This always took place on the Sunday morning, and everyone looked forward to it because as we worked mother would serve us with lashings of beer and rum hotpot. I never knew the proper recipe but it was made with mild draught beer, rum, eggs, milk and ginger. By golly, it was good, and not only as a drink. It was as good as a meal, and you could work on it on a cold day.

Then there were the pigs to be killed and these had to be good and fat too because a lot of lard was needed for Christmas. The bladders of the pigs and the bullocks were emptied, blown up like balloons and hung up to dry. Then when the lard was cooked it was poured into the bladders and was sold, by the bladder, at Christmas for the housewives to use making their mince pies, sausage rolls and so on.

Poultry was the last to be killed and what a job this was. We used to bung up the big holes in the shed with straw to keep out the cold winds, and then the feathers would fly. Just before midnight we used to stop and sort the feathers – the long wing and tail feathers used to be put separately from the short, fluffy ones and sacked up. After Christmas the big coarse feathers would be burnt on a bonfire but the small ones would be sold to make feather beds and cushions.

By this time carcasses hung everywhere, along with the great brown hams we had been curing and smoking since October. It used to take two days to deliver this mountain of meat and poultry, starting very early in the morning until late on Christmas Eve, just about knocking off in time to get a drink before the pubs closed.

For this job the pony cart used to be brought out of the shed and two of us would load this up and make any number of trips. The other two would have great baskets of meat on the

carrier cycles and push them around the village. All the poultry we delivered intact – no birds were ever drawn for our customers. In those days housewives and cooks in domestic service were skilled in this job – they preferred to do it themselves.

During these two days of delivering we would be offered mince pies and home-made wines by our customers almost at every door, and this was the start of our Christmas festivities. Some of our staff one year – I won't mention any names – had more home-made wines than they could take and ended up by driving Bess the pony into the ditch and overturning the cart and all its contents!

Christmas Day

Every Christmas for years and years we had a special guest for dinner, tea and supper. His name was Jack 'Chitty' Reeve.
He was rather a simple-minded chap, a bachelor who lived by himself in the ruins of an old cottage in Bushel Lane. Only one room was waterproof and in this Jack kept an old pram he always pushed about the village to collect his shopping, or to cart the many items people gave him. He was always polite and clean and wore big brown boots that were always shiny. Although he was almost a tramp, he got on well with everyone and is still remembered with affection.

Jack's father was a very successful butcher in Soham many years ago, but died when Jack was very young. So my father always had Jack for Christmas with us because, he used to say, 'Poor old Jack has known better times but has come down in the world.'

Every Christmas morning our guest would arrive, all washed and polished, hair combed and flattened out with Aqua-Pumpi and a coloured handkerchief knotted around his neck. Father would say, 'We'd better have one now, hadn't we,

Snowdrifts in Burwell in the 1920s

Jack,' and Jack was never heard to refuse. So the beer would
flow at dinner, father would carve the joint and put large slices
on Jack's plate, and mother would pile on the vegetables and a
couple of acres of Yorkshire pudding and lashings of rich
gravy. After that came the Christmas puddings that mother
always used to make herself, black as coal and boiled all day in
the same copper she used to boil the linen on washdays.

Then Jack would curl up on the rug by the kitchen fire and
sleep it off while the rest of the family sat in the armchairs to
have a snooze. When tea-time came Jack would come up to the
trough again, and again at supper-time. After a few beers
during the evening, and before leaving to go down the lane to
his humble home, he always used to do a tap dance for us. His
great brown boots used to bang on the lino-covered boarded
floor in our living-room, and the ornaments on the shelves
would do a jig in time with him as he cavorted like a
cart-horse. But he enjoyed himself.

21

Christmas Dinners that Walked to London

DANIEL DEFOE

Though some came to favour roast beef, particularly in Victorian times, turkey was well established as a Christmas dish by the sixteenth century. Flocks of turkeys were kept in Suffolk and Norfolk, including the northern Fen country around King's Lynn and the Wash. As late as the eighteenth century both turkeys and geese were driven to London during the autumn on foot. In A Tour Through the Whole Island of Great Britain *(1724), Daniel Defoe reports on their long march from East Anglia to the markets of the capital.*

I cannot omit, however little it may seem, that this county of Suffolk is particularly famous for furnishing the City of London and all the counties round with turkeys, and that it is thought that there are more turkeys bred in this county, and the part of Norfolk that adjoins it, than in all the rest of England.

On this account I could not omit it, nor will it be found so inconsiderable an article as some may imagine if this be true which I received an account of from a person living in the

place, viz: that they have counted 300 droves of turkeys (for they drive them all in droves on foot) pass in one season . . . on the road to London. These droves, as they say, contain from three hundred to a thousand each drove, so that one may suppose them to contain 500 one with another, which is 150,000 in all.

For the further supplies for the markets of London with poultry, of which these counties particularly abound, they have within these few years found it practicable to make the geese travel on foot too, as well as the turkeys, and a prodigious number are brought up to London in droves from the farthest parts of Norfolk, even from the Fen country about Lynn, Downham, Wisbech and the Washes, as also from all the east side of Norfolk and Suffolk of whom it is very frequent now to meet droves with a thousand, sometimes two thousand in a drove.

They begin to drive them generally in August, by which time the harvest is almost over and the geese may feed in the stubbles as they go. Thus they hold on to the end of October when the roads begin to be too stiff and deep for their broad feet and short legs to march in.

Besides these methods of driving the creatures on foot, they have of late also invented a new method of carriage, being carts formed on purpose with four stories or stages to put the creatures in one above the other by which invention one cart will carry a very great number, and for the smoother going, they drive with two horses abreast, like a coach, so quartering the road for the ease of the gentry that thus ride; changing horses they travel night and day, so that they bring fowls 70, 80 or 100 miles in two days and one night.

The horses in this new-fashioned *Voiture* go two-abreast, as above, but no perch below, as a coach, but they are fastened together by a piece of wood lying crosswise upon their necks by which they are kept even together, and the driver sits on top of his cart, like as in the public carriages for the army.

In this manner they hurry away the creatures alive, and infinite numbers are thus carried to London every year. This method is also particular for the carrying of young turkeys, or turkey poults in their season, which are valuable, and yield a good price at market, as also for live chickens in the dear seasons, of all which a very great number are brought in this manner to London, and more prodigiously out of this country than from any other part of England.

In Memory of a Turkey

H.R.P. OF ELY

In 1913 Mr Cobb of Ely had hoped to dine on turkey but had to make do with ribs of beef. H.R.P.'s poem, the full title of which was 'In Memory of a Turkey who Caught a Chill and Died Two Days Before Christmas', appeared in the Ely Standard.

Proud Stranger, as this modest stone you spy
(Mark how the sculptured sausage greets the eye)
Arrest your footsteps and with me beguile
A tedious moment with a tearful smile.

24

· *A Fenland Christmas* ·

Here deep 'm'd the shadows entombed lies
All that was perfect in the gourmet's eyes.
The praise and wonder of a countryside
At once the hopes, at once the family's pride.

A bird without a peer, so strutted he
With all the attributes of majesty.
Even Mr Cobb, accounted oft a 'rum stick',
Had praised and praised again each fattening drum-
stick.

And when the Zephyr toying with the down
Exposed each gleaming flank, here white, here
bluey-brown
There rose into the circumbient air
A gracious prelude to rich Christmas fare.

But the North wind, full envious as of yore,
Had shot a bolt, and stricken, sudden sore
Poor Paragon, with toes upturned and stiffy,
Had paid his debt to fate in less than half a jiffy.

And on that Christmas Day, poor Cobb with grief,
Dined not on turkey, but on ribs of beef.
A moral, friend, is never to be wasted
Count not your turkeys till you see 'em basted.

Wisbech Christmas Show

'Show Night', held about a week before Christmas, used to be a great occasion in Fenland towns. Shoppers turned out in force and shopkeepers put on extravagant displays to draw in the crowds, with butchers traditionally the main attraction. This 1895 newspaper report gives a lively impression of Show Night in Wisbech nearly a hundred years ago.

Christmas comes this year, not in its old-fashioned guise of frost and snow, but with bright and genial weather. It was hardly possible to imagine old Father Christmas with his red furred cape and long white beard being amongst us with such climatic conditions until we turned out on Wednesday night to do the rounds of the shops. We then soon realized that the gay and festive season had indeed come round. The shops had put on their brightest appearance and on every hand there were signs that Christmas 1895 in this good old town of Wisbech will be as merry as any of its predecessors.

Christmas comes round this year with improved trade and the crowded streets on Wednesday night testified to the heartiness with which the season is hailed. The tradespeople have made ample preparation for a busy Christmas, and the general opinion is that a better Christmas Show has never been seen.

Wisbech Christmas meat market in the 1930s

· *A Fenland Christmas* ·

The butchers' shops, of course, were the main attraction. Mr T. Tansley of High Street, the purchaser of the fine oxen which carried off the Corporation Cup at our Fat Stock Show, again occupied premier position. Nearly all the beasts he had purchased had carried off honours in the prize-giving, and his Southdowns, selected from the flocks of such well-known breeders as HRH the Prince of Wales, were pictures of their kind.

His decorations too were most effective. There was a large star of gas jets over the shop front, and the framework of the window and door were covered with evergreens. On one side of the window there was a giant hind quarter of prime beef, and on the other a fine young deer. The windows of the shop looked most picturesque by gaslight. On one side hung the choice young Southdown from the Prince of Wales' flock and on the other side six prime fat pigs with monster hind-quarters of beef surmounted by the motto 'Merry Christmas To All' at the back.

Mr J.S. Johnson had over his shop front a large and appropriate motto 'Eat, Drink and Be Merry', and in the centre of the window hung a large bullock's head. Mr George Tansley showed his large stock of meat, including eighty quarters of beef, thirty sheep, five lambs, seven pigs and a calf, in a monster tent erected on the Market Hill.

Next to the butchers come the grocers and they spared no efforts in providing good things for the festive board. Mr Crosshill again took the lead for decorative effects. The interior of his shop by gaslight was more like a fairy glen than the emporium of an egg and butter merchant. Messrs Dawbarn and Co. had a luncheon table set out in their window, and Messrs Dowson and Co., in addition to a choice assortment of foreign fruits, stoned, showed a number of fine geese and turkeys.

Among the confectioners Mr Harry Hockney occupied

Locals playing ice hockey on the canal at Wisbech in the 1920s

premier position. The first window in which there was a mechanical figure at work, was set apart for bonbons and fancy packets and boxes of sweetmeats and proved a great attraction to the young folks. In the second window stood a fine wedding cake and a number of Christmas cakes decorated in an elaborate style. The feature of the third window was a gigantic loaf surmounted by a portrait of the employer of the bakehouse.

Thus the tradespeople have done their best towards making Christmas of 1895 a happy one. There is no particular distress in the town and everything points to the tradespeople having a very busy time up to Christmas Day.

Christmas Treats

BLANCHE LOOKER

According to the Wisbech Standard, *then, there was 'no particular distress in the town' in 1895. Out in the Fens, though, conditions were harsher. Blanche Looker was brought up on East Fen Common, outside the village of Soham, around the turn of the century. She talked to Michael Rouse about her memories of Christmas as a child.*

We never had a Christmas tree, we had a Christmas line. A piece of string was put up from one side of the room to the other. We only had one room downstairs, so it had to be out of the way. Little sugar mice and watches and suchlike were hung up there and we were blindfolded and held up to get our Christmas treat from the line — we thought that was lovely.

We didn't have jellies or anything of that sort, but we had bread and butter and jam and cake, which we didn't have in the ordinary way. That was our Christmas. I think mother might have cooked a chicken, but we didn't have meat as children, we just didn't. Mind you, the shops would be open until twelve at night before Christmas. They had stalls outside like a market and naptha flares hung on them. Leonard's the butchers had a sucking pig with an orange stuck in its mouth; I felt sorry about that, I recall. The pubs closed at ten o'clock in the evening and that is often when the women got their money, so a lot of shopping was done after ten.

· A Fenland Christmas ·

Another evening, perhaps it was two evenings before Christmas, every year we made some sweets. There was an oven attached to the open fireplace. Mother had a big stone jar and she'd pop in there two pounds of moist sugar and half a pound of dairy butter – that was her one extravagance. It would be in there all day long, melting and bubbling in the slow oven by the fire.

When we settled down for the evening, mother and I, we had to grease our hands with butter and dip them into the pot – it was boiling hot, that's why we buttered our hands. We would make butter balls, put them all on a tin, and then we'd roll some long ones – it took us almost the whole evening and they were our Christmas sweets, our treat. What a happy memory, sitting there in the lamplight just with my dear mother, peace and quiet, rolling those rich, dark, crumbly sweets for Christmas Day.

Something many people looked forward to at Christmas was the chapel concert and prizegiving. I always had a prize and I used to sing and recite wholesale.

There was a lady in Soham who took a great interest in the Sunday school. She played the harmonium and knew I could sing. When she was putting on these concerts she always wanted me to do something. Well I could never come up to practices because I lived right at the back of beyond, outside the village on East Fen Common, nearly up to Loftus Bridge, so I couldn't come out at night. But somehow or another she would keep me back after Sunday school and she would teach me something to perform.

This particular time we were going to have a concert and prizegiving with a bun and an orange. Mother would come and all the people off the Common. Well Miss Elsdon wanted me to take part in this concert – I'd got to be the sixth part of a rainbow. They had these wooden hoops cut in half and decorated. As I learnt my song, I started singing at home.

Village entertainment in the 1920s – Mr Postlethwaite and his
travelling cinema outside Guyhirn vicarage

'What's that you're singing?' mother says. I was crafty because
I'd got to have a new dress – a flowery dress. I hadn't got one,
I'd never had one – all my dresses had to be serviceable. So I
kept singing my little piece.

'Mother . . .'

'Now what?'

'I've got to have a new dress.'

'New dress! Are you quite out of your mind? This isn't the
anniversary and it isn't the feast, what are you talking about a
new dress for?'

'Well, mother,' I said, 'I've learnt my piece for the Sunday
school concert and I'm going to be part of the rainbow, and it's
got to be a pretty frock, it's got to be a flowery frock.'

'Girl, you're mad,' she says, 'and you can't have a frock,
that's final. Is that what you've been going around the house
singing for?'

· A Fenland Christmas ·

'Yes, I've been practising because I can't go out at night.'

'No, that's final, out of the question,' she said. 'A flowery dress would be no good to you. Whoever heard of such a thing. That's finished.'

'It isn't,' I thought. So I still went on for a few days singing away.

This night we were sitting there and mother said, 'Blanche, I've been thinking . . .' I knew she would come up with something. 'You know that bedroom window upstairs, that little one that nobody ever goes past? I think I could do something with those curtains.'

Of course she hadn't got a machine, but I remember her saying she could 'cobble' it up with big stitches so she could unpick it afterwards. It was material we called madras muslin, cream with yellow roses. Mother put a bit of starch in and I got one curtain in front, one behind, joined up at the shoulders, with a ribbon round the waist. There wasn't a prouder girl in this town. It had got no sleeves but it was beautiful.

When we got to the Christmas concert all the people from the Common were there. It was such a great day for us. Then it came time for me to be the sixth part of a rainbow. I remember sailing all the way down the Sunday school and the VIPs were sitting on one side. As I went past I heard the daughter of one of them say, 'Oh, look at Blanche Goose. Looks as if her frock was made out of her mother's curtains.'

My ego was shattered, but quick as lightning I stuck my tongue out and said, 'It was me they asked to sing, not you.' She couldn't sing; I could. So off I went. I flounced round with my curtains and went on to this big rostrum. I waved my rainbow:

> See across the sky,
> Beyond the clouds on high,
> A rainbow, a beautiful rainbow . . .

33

A winter's day in the Fens – Twenty Pence Ferry in the 1920s

I'd never sung like it before, nor have I since. I was so proud of my frock and she had said that. I was angry too because mother had taken all that trouble to please me and let me sing.

That party was our Christmas treat. And we had our prizes. I had some beautiful books, as I learnt my scripture. At the end of the evening we had a bun and an orange. Then we lit the lanterns with the candles in for going home. There were no street lights then and with mother with us we went bumping all over town as we made our way home out along the river bank wrapped against the December cold.

Christmas Advertising, Victorian Style

The approach of Christmas can turn shopkeepers into poets. Take S. Sheldon, for instance, proprietor of a 'General Fancy Repository' in Petty Cury, Cambridge, who put this lyrical advertisement in her local newspaper in December 1868.

Another Year is nearly past,
Another Christmas coming fast:
S. SHELDON, as she's done before,
Has much increased her usual store
Of Goods to suit the festive season,
And hopes her friends will give her reason
To thank them every one and all,
For well responding to her call.
At her Establishment you'll find
Varieties of every kind,
At prices no one can think high
Or elsewhere can so cheaply buy.
Writing Desks, useful, strong and good,
Mahogany, walnut and rosewood
Papier-Mâché in good store,
Ink stands, blotters and much more.

· A Fenland Christmas ·

A well-selected stock of Toys
Suited alike for Girls or Boys.
Games and Puzzles out of number,
To keep the young ones' eyes from slumber.
Bricks in boxes, Dominoes,
Dolls arrayed in gorgeous clothes.
And Pa and Ma should now remember,
These things are wanted this December.
When little ones leave school behind,
These are the things they like to find.
Every article for Berlin Work,
Cushions, Ottomans, or Cap of Turk.
An Extensive choice for Christmas Trees,
Which Old and Young are sure to please.

*　　*　　*

*T. Waltham, Baker, Confectioner, Pastry Cook and
Sugar Boiler of Bedford Street, Wisbech, wished his
customers 'A Merry Christmas and a Prosperous New
Year' in 1891 with this little ode.*

Oh! say, have you heard the news of late,
About the candy man so great,
Who places the town in such a state,
By selling wonderful candy, oh!

I say, the people of this town,
The people of Wisbech tell me so,
They would freely go ten miles or more,
For an ounce of Waltham's Candy, oh!

Now, Janie, when your work is done,
Up to the Market you may run,

36

But be sure and call at Waltham's stall,
And bring back a pound of sweets for us all.

Yes, Madam, that is my delight,
Their stall is always nice and bright,
And those that give him a Christmas call,
He'll try to satisfy them all.

T. WALTHAM HAS SOME
SPLENDID WREATHS AND BASKETS MADE FROM
SUGAR
which will be suitable for Presents

*   *   *

*Burrall Bros, agents for the Silverbowl Tea Company,
went for drama in their advertising rather than poetry.
This fast-moving tale appeared in the* Wisbech Standard
on Christmas Day, 1891.

A BRAVE DEED

He knew the crowd he had to deal with

Madly flew the sleigh over the trackless prairies. The
bloodcurdling howls of the wolves that grew momentarily
nearer and nearer lent wings to the panting animals, and they
tore along over the snowy wastes, every muscle strained to its
utmost, every nerve quivering, their nostrils dilated, their eyes
starting from their sockets, and long trails of filmy vapour
from their steaming bodies trailing in their wake.

'Comrades,' said one of the men in the sleigh, rising up,
pale, but with iron resolution within every line of his face, 'the
wolves are gaining upon us. If we had ten minutes we could
reach the farmhouse yonder, but we cannot do it. There is only

one hope. One of us must sacrifice himself for the others. Farewell.' Before they could stop him he had thrown himself out of the sleigh and disappeared. On flew the horses. The sleigh, relieved of the weight of the brave man who had voluntarily offered himself as a sacrifice, went perceptibly faster. A few moments later they dashed into the yard surrounding the little farmhouse. They were saved!

But how had it fared with that dauntless, unselfish hero? Will it be believed? The gaunt, hungry wolves, diverted from the pursuit of the sleigh, had no sooner surrounded him than they seemed to regard him as a friend. They fawned upon him with every demonstration of delight, and one of the boldest and finest of the whole pack offered him his paw as if to shake hands with him, shook his head slowly, turned about and trotted away, followed by all the rest.

The fierce, bloodcurdling wolves had recognized this man as a kindred spirit.

He was a traveller for the world-renowned SILVERBROOK TEA COMPANY, blenders of the finest teas in the world.

Agents for Wisbech
BURRALL BROS

Seasonable Suggestions

In 1896 the Wisbech Standard *took this light-hearted look at Christmas presents, both giving and receiving. A hundred years ago, it seems, Japanese blue and white china was all the rage.*

Don'ts for Christmastide

Don't wilfully deprive your children of belief in Santa Claus. It is hard enough for older people to get along without him.

Don't give a present designed as a missionary offer. Soap is an excellent thing but as a gift it might give offence.

Don't give a friend cheap jewellery. After the first glad surprise and gold-plate has worn off, you may lose a friend.

Don't attempt to make the small boy who expects a pair of skates believe that an overcoat is more consistent with his highest good.

Don't forget, if you are buying a gift for a girl who needs a warm wrap, that a hand-painted plaque never kept anyone from freezing.

Don't purchase a costly article solely for the purpose of laying its recipient under obligation. This is a political method not favoured in private life.

Don't wait till the last to get presents for those you care about most. The money may give out at any time.

Don't forget, if your salary is paid on the 1st, that between December 25th and that date there is a week, during which it is necessary to live.

Givers of Gifts Should Remember:

That uselessness is not synonymous with attractiveness.

That the mother of the family has not entirely outgrown the feminine fondness for pretty things.

That the father cannot be expected to grow enthusiastic over a gift of lace curtains for the parlour.

That a bald-headed man will probably take umbrage if presented with a pair of brushes bearing his monogram.

That it is as well to learn the size of a woman's hand before sending her a box of gloves.

Those who Receive Gifts Should Remember:

That it is still in bad taste to look a gift horse in the mouth.

That the hideous clock sent by the rich relative from whom one has expectations must be given a place of honour in one's home.

That there is always the blessed possibility of exchanging duplicates.

That it is not friendly to search for price tags nor to carry one's gifts to the shops to learn their value.

That it is not evidence of high Christian merit to cross from one's visiting list the names of all who have failed to send one Christmas tokens.

· A Fenland Christmas ·

Christmas cards and calendars in a Wisbech shop window in
the 1930s

Presents for a Child

A locomotive and four coaches in iron.
Swing to be suspended from the ceiling.
A small tin range with cooking utensils.
Tallyho coach that runs automatically.
A large box of Greenaway writing paper.
Organ-grinder and his outfit in miniatures.
A nail-file in silver that closes up like a knife.
A little pen-holder, inkstand and desk blotter.
Box of tools large enough to be serviceable.
School bag of stout canvas with leather initials.
A box containing half a dozen small fine handkerchiefs.

A large Noah's ark, with the family and the animals.
A case of modelling apparatus with clay ready for use.
A fleet of small vessels which follow a magnet in the water.
A knife, fork and spoon of white metal with Dresden handles.

Presents for a Woman

Square floral portrait frames in coloured enamel.
Manicure pieces in good steel, with plated handles.
Six Japanese blue and white bread and butter plates.
Set of lace and muslin collar-tabs and turned back cuffs.
Satin pin-cushion with Honiton lace square across top.
A Japanese blue and white sugar basin and cream jug.
Small plated fern dish for the centre of the dining table.
Two fine towels with drawn work borders.
Set of small round-headed silver hat pins of assorted sizes.
Small carefully-selected bottle of perfumery or toilet water.
Japanese blue and white salt cellars, pepper holders and trays.
Four Japanese blue and white afternoon tea cups and saucers.
Three Japanese blue and white oatmeal bowls with saucers to
    match.
Cut-glass olive tray, rose bowl, small chrysanthemum vase or
    flower holder.
Tray, candlestick, ring-holder, glove box or powder box of
    polished red cedar.

Saving Time on Christmas Shopping

By the 1960s Christmas shopping had become an altogether more serious affair. In December 1967 Cambridgeshire and Peterborough Life provided their readers with lots of gift ideas, complete with prices and where in the region to buy them.

Men

Christmas should always start with a laugh so why not get the ball rolling with a brightly coloured nightshirt which is virtually a long shirt – known in the trade as a sleep coat (69/6, Ellis Bell, Peterborough). If your husband or boyfriend is too modest you can settle for a pair of modern and brightly patterned Hardy Amies pyjamas (from 63/–, Bodger & Co, Cambridge).

Men, although never admitting it, are vain creatures, so how about pampering him with a velvet jacket (£14, Bodger), a suede fronted cardigan (£8.18.6d, W. Sutterby and Gay, Wisbech) or a superbly designed and quite startling quilted dressing gown (6 gns, Ellis Bell). In the cheaper luxurious range there are attractive cravats (11/6, Ellis Bell), suede ties (1 gn, Sutterby) or a sheepskin hat with ear flaps, ideal for hunting, shooting and fishing (Sutterby).

Having dressed your man he will need something to put his clothes in. A good bet are 'Revelation' or 'Gannex' suitcases

· A Fenland Christmas ·

Christmas shopping in Ely, 1900

(from £4.17.6d, Sutterby). Incidentally 'Gannex' are the people who make the Prime Minister's raincoats.

For the smaller gift I suggest a pair of Jack Brabham driving gloves (52/6d, Ellis Bell), a Shell road atlas (15/–, Robert Sayle, Cambridge), or for the fisherman, a 'Fisherman's Pride' multi-purpose tool including a tape measure and spring balance (Joshua Taylor, Cambridge).

Women

Christmas is a time to give women luxuries – something they wouldn't have bought normally. For that special present jewellery is probably the best item. Flexible gold bracelets, necklets or collarettes (from £30, Charles Bright, Peterborough) would be appreciated. Dress rings (from £10, Charles Bright) would also bring an affectionate 'thank you'.

Out of the ordinary furniture would please any house-

Snow falls on Cambridge market, 1980s

proud woman. Wicker shell chairs (£3.19.11d, W. Thompson & Sons, Cambridge) or attractive dressing table stools (£7.16s, Peak's Furniture, Cambridge) would fit in the bedroom easily.

A surprise piece of clothing always brings a good response from a woman. A stretch fur hat to fit any size head (£4.10s, Sutterby), a mohair stole (32/11, John Bryant, St Ives), a Nurse's sheepskin coat (£27.10s, Sutterby), or even a needlecord skirt to keep you warm (39/6, Robert Sayle) all come into this category.

Finally there are two expensive luxuries that are just asking to be bought. Firstly the Ronson electric toothbrush (11 gns, Shelton's, Peterborough) to really get those teeth pearly white, and secondly the Hawkins Teasmade (£22.10s, Shelton's). The Teasmade's alarm will wake you up with the tea all ready to drink. What more could you ask from luxury?

45

Christmas lights in Petty Cury, Cambridge, 1960s

Teenagers

I always think teenagers are the easiest people to buy Christmas presents for. Clothes are always appreciated by the growing young man. A silk cravat or a wool tie (35/– and from 7/6d, Bodger) are ideal.

If you would like to cut a very smart figure a good idea are the very artistic-looking needlecord corduroy jackets (10 gns, Ellis Bell).

A useful present for both sexes is the Looping or Imhof quality Swiss travelling clock to get them out of bed on time (from 6 gns, Charles Bright) or a beech and canvas safari chair (£9.19s, Thorpe Design House, Peterborough).

Finally for the teenage girl, there is the evergreen present of

underwear. This year you can really give her something to go to town over. In brilliant floral patterns and other bright designs you can buy matching sets consisting of bra, panties, slips and girdles (£2.10s, Robert Sayle).

Children

Christmas belongs to children and as usual the shops have done them proud. But this year it looks as if parents are going to pay out a lot more money than last year because there are so many presents they will have trouble resisting. Every father will want his son to have an electric motor racing kit even if his son never gets a chance to play with it (from £4.2.3d, Eaden Lilley, Cambridge). Also in the expensive range are Mini pedal cars and pedal trains (£8.19.6d and £14.19.11d, Peaks).

Lowering the price a bit there are still some fascinating gifts. Presents like a Mettoy typewriter (27/6d, Eaden Lilley), battery operated vacuum cleaners (63/–, Joshua Taylor), or Manquette covered armchairs for kids (£5.19.6d, Joshua Taylor).

Bendy toys – models of characters like Sooty and Yogi Bear that can be bent into any position – are a good example of cheaper toys (from 12/11d, R.J. Glass, Peterborough). You can also buy a doll that cries, drinks, sleeps and wets her nappies (Peak's).

Two last suggestions are one of the Waddington's games and an object called a Ride-a-Roo (49/11d, Joshua Taylor) which is an inflatable jockey ball which children can ride around on.

Peterborough Cathedral's Silent Christmas Bells

TREVOR A. BEVIS

Here is a story with a happy ending. In 1972 local historian Trevor Bevis wrote this piece about the bells of Peterborough Cathedral, which had not been rung in the traditional manner for many years. Today the cathedral has a fine ring of twelve bells, while Henry Penn's original tenor bell still sounds occasionally from the north-west tower.

Christmas is a season of noise. Noise reverberating from the streets, shops and markets. Noise pouring from churches and chapels in ancient tradition seeking to remind the worldly-minded what Christmas is all about. Loud organs play at full swell the glories of the Christ Child; bells take up the message and disperse it over the frosty air to merry homes far and near.

Now there's a point. Of all the Christmassy noises repeated every twelve months, none is more magical or more closely associated with the festive season than the sound of bells. To enjoy Christmas without bells is like devouring the turkey without a pinch of salt.

Many times the writer has parked his posterior on a

well-worn, 800-year-old step leading into the south aisle of Peterborough Cathedral. Habitually he unwraps his sandwiches beneath the Norman arch, observing the changing of the seasons in the fern, the grass and distant trees. And through it all – at precisely 1 p.m. – the great bell of the north-west tower, a deep, sonorous tenor, spells out the time to the luncher.

I have often tried to imagine the rhythm of changes from the old ring of ten bells cascading above the market place on the occasions of Georgian Christmas preludes. It hasn't happened at Peterborough for more than a century and it may never happen again.

Peterborough Cathedral stands on the edge of fenland, one of Europe's grandest Norman/Early English monuments, whose west front portrays the best conception of ancient Greece embodied in the Christian language. Immediately to the rear of the left gabled arch rises a pinnacled tower containing five near-redundant bells – all that remains of a noble ring of ten. Within this tower and, to a lesser degree within its companion adjoined to the south aisle, bells for centuries past called the faithful to Christmas services.

Earliest records of bells relate to the thirteenth century when Pope Gregory granted bells to the monks of Peterborough. In 1250 the bells were augmented by Johannes Caleto, abbot, and a few years later the towers were erected under the jurisdiction of abbot Richardus of London who gave two bells inscribed 'Les Londres'.

As required by the authors of the Dissolution, an inventory of the cathedral's effects took place, dated 30 November 1539: 'In the chappel of Low – Item 3 bells to ring in the chappel. In the infirmary chappel, Item one little bell. Item in the two steeples of the monastery at the Front, bells 10, and in several other places of the House, bells, 4.'

One assumes that only a few of the ten bells mentioned

hung in the south-west tower, which remains to this day incomplete and almost indiscernible from the main gateway. Due to unsettled foundations the thirteenth-century builders abandoned the third stage.

The infirmary bells were sold soon after the inventory, but the tower bells were allowed to remain. Cromwell's soldiers amused themselves during their stay in the city and occasionally playfully jangled the bells. Some say the Ironsides removed the bells' clappers and sold them together with brass plucked from the tombs. In fact, the city's inhabitants removed the clappers and hid them in the nave roof to free their ears of irritating and frequently intrusive chiming.

The bells often rang in the late-seventeenth century and in 1665 the ringers received five shillings for ringing the news of the overthrow of the Dutch fleet. Ten 'great' bells continued in service until 1709 in which year they were removed.

The five bells surviving today were cast by Henry Penn, Peterborough's only founder of note. His foundry was on the south side of Bridge Street, approached by a dyke from the Nene upon which barges conveyed bells from various regions.

Penn was said to be 'a vile man; his death was no loss for he gave trouble wheresoever he was concerned'. Yet he was a good founder who gave a benefactory of £50 towards adorning the cathedral's higher altar.

He had cast a ring of bells for St Ives parish church, but the townspeople were dissatisfied with the peal and a tedious lawsuit followed. Finally it was decided in favour of Penn who had ridden from Peterborough to St Ives to be present at the Huntingdonshire Assizes. Unfortunately, as he was mounting his horse in the inn yard at St Ives to return to Peterborough, he fell down dead from overexcitement.

Henry Penn's ten bells occupied the belfry of the north-west tower. They were rung for about 120 years, until an architect expressed fears that the vibrations were endangering the West

front. In 1831 the first five bells were sold to William Dobson, a capable founder of Downham Market who cast a new ring of six bells from Peterborough's five for Witham-on-the-Hill.

Not unnaturally, a large number of the city's inhabitants were dismayed when Penn's bells were reduced to a meagre five. Regret was expressed that the bells of Peterborough Cathedral were not rung in the traditional manner. Eventually it was agreed that the remaining five bells be quarter-turned and re-hung in a steel frame at a cost of £300. Several ringers from far and near arrived at the cathedral to re-open the bells after their restoration. One, the late Mr A.J. Abrams of Chatteris cycled the 56 mile round trip on his penny-farthing.

This fine old Fenman claimed to have been the last person to have rung the tenor bell. The occasion was a 'double'. The wedding in the cathedral of a well-known couple was a good excuse to ring the bells and word had been passed round the campanological fraternity that Penn's bells would be available for ringing on that particular afternoon.

The architect was listening and watching, however, and that afternoon's activities convinced him that the famous west front could not survive repeated dosages. The location of the five heavy bells on one side of the tower may well have set the tower 'rocking' excessively, so much so that the west front would be under some strain.

Since then it would seem the bells have remained quite still, their stays and ropes removed. They are sounded by vergers who 'string' them through the medium of a chiming apparatus in the north aisle. Of good casting, the bells occupy their original bays, alongside the empty spaces formerly occupied by their unwanted companions.

It may be that in future years Peterborough Cathedral will adopt an additional role as parish church. If that day should come, one can only hope that bells in full swing will be heard ringing from the tower of this very lovely building.

Meanwhile, with the approach of another Christmas, one confidently expects to hear the traditional message pealing above the rapidly changing face of the city from the towers of St John's and St Mary's nearby: Happy and peaceful Christmas.

Cambridge to Ely by Mail Coach

On 14 November 1989 a horse-drawn Royal Mail coach, the only stagecoach still licensed to carry mail, pulled away from King's Parade in Cambridge, bound for Ely. Tourists, press photographers and passers-by watched as the guard blew his bugle, and driver John Parker cracked his whip. The four white horses had waited calmly amid all the fuss. Now they were off. On board, in Victorian dress, were the Dean of Ely Cathedral, Head Postmaster Tony Begley, artist David Gentleman and his young son, together with two BBC Radio Cambridgeshire listeners who had won the ride in a competition. Following the 1840s mail coach with its 1980s police escort was a large Post Office 'Write It' exhibition bus.

The occasion was the launch of the 1989 Christmas stamp issue, five special designs created by David Gentleman to mark the 800th anniversary of the completion of the massive Norman nave of Ely cathedral.

· *A Fenland Christmas* ·

The 1840s Royal Mail coach driven by John Parker, who is
well wrapped up against the cold

Ely's original Saxon church was destroyed by the Danes in
the ninth century. After the Norman conquest William
appointed Simeon as Abbot of Ely. Though well into his
eighties by this time, Simeon set about organizing the
building of a new church with great energy. In 1189, more
than a century later, the masons and carpenters and other
dedicated craftsmen, working with little more than simple
hand tools, finally completed their awesome task. Ely's
magnificent cathedral, one of the finest pieces of medieval
architecture in Europe, soared proudly, then as now, towering
over the surrounding Fens.

David Gentleman's Christmas stamp designs show some of
the intricate detail adorning Ely's great monument to English
architecture. On arriving at the cathedral, the artist unveiled a
stained glass version of the 15p stamp, specially commissioned
for the anniversary celebrations.

· *A Fenland Christmas* ·

The Dean of Ely Cathedral helps show off the 1989 Christmas
stamps

By today's standards the journey had been long and cold.
Cambridge to Ely is only sixteen miles – less than half an hour
by car, and though John Parker's fine Hungarian horses are
sturdy and willing, the Royal Mail coach cannot travel at more
than seven miles an hour.

In their heyday these coaches would carry up to four
passengers together with the mail. What is striking when you
look inside is how small they are. Large people can't have been
popular and even average-sized passengers wouldn't have had
much knee- or elbow-room.

Not that such coaches carried Christmas mail as we know it.
The first Christmas card appeared in 1843 but it was only in
the 1870s that the custom of sending cards really began to take
off. The first time the Christmas mail was thought worthy of a
mention in the annual report of the Post Office was in 1878,

54

when they handled four and a half million letters. By this time, however, mail was increasingly being carried by rail.

Not only were a limited number of official first day covers carried on the 1989 commemorative mail-coach run, the Ely Christmas stamps were remarkable for another reason: that year, for the first time, the Post Office invited customers to pay an extra 1p on four of the five stamps, the money raised to go to charity. The public's response meant that more than half a million pounds was raised, so that the celebration of 800 years of Ely Cathedral's history brought benefits far beyond the Fens.

Goodening Day

MABEL DEMAINE

On St Thomas' Day, 21 December, poor widows, and sometimes widowers, in Cambridgeshire villages used to do the rounds of their more prosperous neighbours collecting money and small gifts for Christmas. In some villages the custom extended to all old people. Variously known as Goodening (or Gooding) Day, Gathering Day or Mumping Day, the tradition lasted into the early years of this century, as Mabel Demaine of Haddenham recalls.

When I was a child widows went round on Goodening Day. I don't know how it originated but on 21 December, the

shortest day of the year, widows in ones and twos went around knocking on doors, where they were given small sums of money or a packet of tea or sugar.

Only widows were allowed to take part in this, but one year old Jinny Croxen joined the collectors. We all knew she wasn't a widow, though it was true her husband was often ill and unable to work.

When she came to our house her right to join the widows was challenged and she promptly replied: 'I'm wors'en a widow woman!'

Widows were really poor in those days and had a hard life. There were no pensions and often their poverty was acute. Sometimes they got some small 'parish relief', a mere pittance, and it meant pleading poverty and almost begging, and these women had their pride.

I remember one woman who was left a widow with an invalid daughter to keep. She went out washing and became almost bent double through bending over the washtub – there was hard scrubbing to be done, then the ironing, a full hard day several times a week – no washing-machines or electric irons in those days. We used to see her going home, her stooping figure looking so tired and weary after these washing days. Goodening Day, coming just before Christmas, provided them with a little extra for the festive season.

The Festival of Carols at King's College

IRENE LISTER

On Christmas Eve in Cambridge a long queue stretches back from the entrance to King's College Chapel, winding its way around the Gibbs building and out towards King's Parade. A few stalwarts at the head of the queue have spent one, sometimes two, nights camping out in the cold to make sure of the best seats. The rest have been gathering since before dawn. For the nine hundred strong congregation the world-famous Festival of Nine Lessons and Carols marks the start of Christmas – as it does for millions more as they listen to the service broadcast live. Irene Lister was a prolific writer on local history. In 1974 she produced this account of the celebrated carol service whose roots go back more than five hundred years.

When Henry the Sixth planned his twin colleges of Eton at Windsor and King's at Cambridge he was only nineteen. Illness had not then clouded his mind, and the Wars of the Roses were still in the future. He could not have imagined that over five centuries later, carols from his wonderfully conceived chapel would be broadcast on Christmas Eve, and

that their message of praise and joy would wing round the world, making glad the hearts of men and women everywhere.

The young Henry laid the foundation stone of the chapel in 1446, having planned the building in all its magnificent detail. He knelt then and said a prayer for his lay clerks and choral singers: his prayer is still used in services today. Perhaps because he was so young himself, he ordained that there should always be sixteen boys to sing as choristers together with men – originally lay clerks and now choral scholars – who are full members of King's College.

Nowadays we hear broadcast the Festival of Nine Lessons and Carols, but in the early times the carols were lyrics set to a dance measure, sometimes being the combination of dance and song. At Christmas the festival would be celebrated with the crib set up in the churches and the congregation dancing and singing the lyric songs telling of the birth of a Child, often accompanied by the performance of 'mystery plays'.

King's College always kept the festival at Christmas, and although Henry's illness together with the wars and an impoverished country prevented the cathedral-sized building from being completed, it is probable that services were held with a temporary covering for a roof. Boy bishops were installed at Christmas in large churches and King's too had a boy bishop who officiated at services from St Nicholas Day (December 6) until Childermas (December 28).

It was the Tudors – Henry VII, then Henry VIII – who contributed finally to complete what is sometimes called 'the finest flower of late Gothic in Europe'. During the 1530s the Chapel was finally ready for full-scale worship. By the time of Orlando Gibbons, a chorister at King's under the charge of an elder brother, music as we know it began to be heard. In the early years of the seventeenth century, Gibbons composed music for a payment of around two shillings a piece. Then

· A Fenland Christmas ·

King's College Chapel in the snow, 1880s

followed a time when choristers were chosen particularly for their voices, as the founder most probably had wished.

Later in the century, however, in Cromwell's time, the Chapel came to be called 'the place of a thousand superstitions'. A black pall seemed to come down over those early joyous and almost pagan festivals held in churches. Everything of a happy nature ceased, it seems, during the Cromwell years. Christmas was at first made a Fast Day and then in 1647 the Long Parliament abolished it entirely along with other festivals.

Yet the Chapel organ whose rich tones are heard by millions over the air was beloved by Milton, who wrote of it:

> There let the pealing organ blow
> To the full-voiced quire below,

· *A Fenland Christmas* ·

In service high and anthems clear,
As may with sweetness through mine ear,
Dissolve me into ecstasies,
And bring all heaven before my eyes.

And so to the present day, when for many Christmas starts
as we listen at 3 p.m. on the Eve to the broadcast service from
King's. One of the boy choristers will begin the service and,
although he is chosen beforehand, it is said that he will not be
told until shortly before the service is due to begin. He will
sing 'Once in Royal David's City' solo, holding each listener
enthralled.

Then comes the Bidding Prayer, not peculiar to univer-
sities, but prescribed in the Canons of 1603 for use before the
sermons and, in King's, derived from ancient local usage.

The solo chorister will begin the Lessons, which afterwards
in turn are read by a choral scholar, the organist, a fellow, the
vice-provost, a Free Churchman, the Mayor's chaplain, a
representative of the sister college at Eton, and finally the
Provost himself: each Lesson telling the tale of our Redemp-
tion, but adapted to symbolise and express the loving bond
between the two foundations of Eton at Windsor and King's
College at Cambridge.

Between each lesson the carols are sung, some being
changed each year, while dimly the light from the great
windows illumines the choristers, each in scarlet cassock and
white surplice. The candles flicker but no longer throw off
carbon, for they contain animal fat these days, not wax.

Over all there is gentle warmth from the underfloor heating,
a comfort that our earlier choristers did not have. But they all
had the advantage of the splendid acoustics, which, as two
cousins who were choral scholars have told me, make it such a
joy to sing there.

And so to the conclusion of this well-loved service, when all

Modern-day King's College choirboys rehearsing in the Chapel

those present in the Chapel will leave feeling fully feasted on the first joys of Christmas.

Epitaph – Henry VI's Prayer:

O Lord Jesus Christ, who hast created and redeemed me, and has brought me hither where I am: Thou knowest what Thou wouldest do with me: do with me according to Thy Will, with mercy. Amen.

Larking and Practical Joking

THOMAS H. CASE

King's College's sixteen boy-choristers weren't always the little angels they appear today. Thomas Case was a chorister from 1836 to 1845. His Memoirs show that you had to be tough to survive as a King's Choir boy in the early Victorian years. As he says in his preface, 'at this date King's Choir boys were not, as a whole, the best specimen of schoolboys . . .'. In 1989 the headmaster of King's College Choir School dressed up as Santa Claus and gave out presents to the young choristers. 150 years earlier, Christmas was a rather less innocent affair.

· A Fenland Christmas ·

Looking very serious – King's College choir in 1901

Several parties were given during the Christmas season, and at these every inducement was presented for a growing liking for drinking and gambling. Wine and cards were important items of enjoyment, and although the 'speculation' was not for large sums (I think my limited allowance at starting from home was one shilling), there was borrowing and staying late.

One boy had friends at Trinity Lodge, and would take a companion frequently on a Sunday morning, just before dinner, on a visit to the Servants' Hall and have some of Dr W——'s ale. Also the Hall Boys had easy access to wine from the King's Combination Room Pantry and from the Fellows' Cellars, in addition to being able to purchase ale (through certain servants) at the College Buttery. The Butteries were equal then to a Pub Bar at certain hours in the day.

The King's Boys were a sort of butt for other sets – and

especially the Pitt Press Boys, who were always in active opposition, sometimes in single combat, sometimes in small companies, and upon certain occasions, especially in a good old 'snow winter', en masse. If the Pitts could be drawn into King's Lane they would have a warm innings as they would have more King's boys to contend with. Cooks and others would not tolerate the row these skirmishes caused.

The Pitts were too strong in number for the King's to be drawn into their territory in Mill Lane, so most of our battles were of a skirmishing order (or disorder). Occasionally there were stand-ups with 'Free School Lane' boys, but it was an unwritten law that when hostilities did break out, the climax was decided between two champions either on Queens' Green, which was Pitt ground, or on Clare Hall Piece, which was ours.

Sing All Ye Merry

JACK OVERHILL

Jack Overhill was a remarkable man: a broadcaster who gave over fifty talks on BBC Radio, a writer with thirty published and unpublished books to his credit, and a keen swimmer who took a daily dip in the River Cam for more than sixty years. He began his working life in his father's trade as a shoemaker. He ended it, after an external degree

· A Fenland Christmas ·

achieved in his forties, teaching economics at the Cambridgeshire College of Arts and Technology. In this Christmas Eve story he recalls his Cambridge childhood before the First World War.

I lived with my father, a shoemaker, and two brothers in a Cambridge cul-de-sac of four-roomed houses before the First World War. There was a little general stores at the end of the street and it was a pleasant pastime to look at the sweets in the window and think what I'd buy if I had a farthing. A week or two before Christmas I always knew what I'd buy – one of the sugar novelties that were decorated with coloured pictures of Father Christmas, church bells, holly and mistletoe.

The sugar novelties were the start of Christmas for me – it was time to look in the big shops and pick out the toys and crackers and Christmas stockings I'd buy if I had the money. It was time to start making paper-chains to decorate the front room. And to go carol-singing.

My father's idea of Christmas was a well-stocked cupboard without getting into debt. He was a good cook and, when trade was brisk, he bought a joint of beef, made a baked pudding and a plum pudding – he put silver threepenny bits in the plum pudding – and mince tarts on dinner plates. He was saved the job of making a cake – the baker always gave us one at Christmas for our yearly custom.

Besides plenty of food, beer had to come into the picture to please my father. He liked a drop o' beer. He talked about it in pints and half-pints and, when he could afford it, that was the way he bought it – more often than not in a jug to drink at home, one of us fetching it from the pub. One day, when he was well off, he was going to buy a four-and-a-half gallon barrel. 'I will, don't damn me,' he'd say. The determination in his voice was like that of a man set on doing a daring deed; but he said it too often to mean it. Well, we thought so; it was just a bit of

'Go to Dale, the brewer, and order me a four-and-a-half.'
Dale's Brewery delivery van, 1920s

make-believe. As if he was likely to spend four-and- sixpence on beer. That was more than the weekly rent of the house we lived in — nearly as much as he got for making a pair of boots.

He did mean it. After breakfast on Christmas Eve he said to my brother Nap: 'Go to Dale, the brewer, and order me a four-and-a-half.'

Nap was fifteen. He had infantile paralysis when he was a child and it had left him with a crippled leg. That hadn't damped his spirit. He could swim and dive and ride a bicycle; and when he walked he swung along at a good pace. He liked to take things to pieces — he was never able to put them together again — and just then he was busy on a clock. He took no notice.

'Do you hear what I say?' said my father.

'Yes, I hear,' said Nap.

'Then do as I say — go and order me a four-and-a-half.'

Nap grinned. 'A four-and-a-half? Why not a niner? Or a thirty-sixer?'

My father took his chaff good-humouredly. 'A four-and-a-half will do.'

'Like me to call at a shop and order a brace o' pheasants at the same time?'

'I don't want any of your old buck. You do as I say.'

Nap still didn't think he was serious. 'You don't mean it, do you?' he said.

'Of course I mean it. Off you go.'

Nap didn't budge.

'Well, what are you wait'n for?'

'The money.'

'Tell 'em cash on delivery.'

'That'll work, that will.'

'Work – of course it'll work, said my father. 'They take beer to worse places than this. I'm not having it on the nod. I'm hav'n it cash on delivery. That's a different thing. Now, do as I say – go 'n order me a four-and-a-half. They'll take the order. Be glad to.'

Nap went then; but not willingly. Going to a place like Dale's on an errand of that sort. A nice job the old man had got him on to. That – and a bit more – was written all over him as he left the house and went to the brewery in Gwydir Street a mile away.

He came back looking more cheerful. 'They'll deliver it this afternoon,' he said.

'There, what did I tell you. They were glad of the order. Could do with a few more like it.' And pleased with himself, my father got on with his work. And while he worked he talked about the four-and-a-half gallon that would soon be delivered. He was already sampling the beer and was obviously feeling very proud of himself for ordering it.

By the middle of the afternoon, he was looking out of the window and listening to every cart in the street. The four-and-a-half was a long time coming. It ought to have been

there by now. Ah, things weren't like they were. Years ago
when a firm took an order they soon carried it out. They
wouldn't have lasted long if they hadn't. He was getting
worked up when there was a knock on the door. It opened. A
voice shouted; 'Anybody in?' And there stood the brewer's
drayman with the four-and-a-half.

There was a touch of ceremony about it when my father paid
him. Then, after wishing the drayman a happy Christmas, he
carried the barrel of beer into the kitchen and almost
reverently placed it on the table.

As it was Christmas Eve, he knocked off early and went out,
leaving me, Nap and Perce, the other one of the family, on our
own. Perce was nine, a bit older than me. He went to the
cupboard and looked at the barrel of beer.

'Here, you leave that alone,' said Nap.

'I'm only looking at it.'

'Ah, I know you.' And Nap nodded to show just how much
he knew him.

They began to argue. But it was a friendly argument and it
ended in their suzzling at the beer-tap.

'Coo, you'll cop it,' I said. And not wanting to get mixed
up in that bit of sacrilege, I went out. I was going out anyway,
carol-singing with one of my mates.

After we'd drawn a blank at several houses, we stopped
outside Stokeslea in Union Road, the home of the Reverend
John William Edward Coneybeare. That seemed a likely place
and we made our usual slow and cautious approach through
the gateway and garden to the front porch. After we'd sung
several carols, or as much as we knew of them, we ended with
our old favourite:

> Sing all ye merry, Christmas is near,
> The day that we all love best, the day of the year;

Local lads building a snowman on Petersfield, Cambridge,
1906

Bring forth the holly, the box and the may,
Decorate your cottage on a fine Christmas day. . . .

We lingered loud and long on the word 'day', and, our
carol-singing over, he thanked us, gave us sixpence, wished us
a merry Christmas, and showed us out.

A tanner to share! It was the luck of a lifetime. We headed
straight for the fish and chip shop in Russell Street. I could
have shouted with joy.

After eating a haporth of juicy chips sprinkled with salt and
vinegar I went home. My father was still out, but Nap and
Perce were there. And they were playing an old trick –
pretending they were asleep. Nap with his head on his arms on
the table and Perce on a chair leaning up against the wall.

'Come on, trying to make out you're asleep,' I said; and I
gave Nap a shake and Perce a push. That should have woken

69

them up. It didn't. Perce only moved slightly and Nap didn't move at all.

I'd show them.

I shook Nap – hard. He moved, but he didn't sit up and laugh as I thought he would; he simply turned his head and mumbled, 'Lemme alone.'

That startled me. So did his slavering manner.

There were two empty glasses on the table. I picked one up and sniffed it. I smelt Nap's breath. I went over to Perce and smelt his. Then I knew the truth, the horrible truth. They were drunk.

I stood, too scared to move. If my father found out he'd go sky high. Suddenly I came to and in a panic I opened the stairs door, got hold of Nap and heaved him out of the chair. Trying to talk sense into him, I got him to the stairs then began pushing him up them. He went slowly, on all fours, because of his condition and his crippled leg.

As soon as he was in the bedroom I went down for Perce. He always bossed me about and he turned awkward when I started to boss him. Somehow I got him to the stairs and bundled him up them.

My father never found out. A jolly good thing he didn't. He was always on about the evil of strong drink. *He* had a glass of beer now and again; but when we grew up we mustn't touch it – *none of us – never*.

Good King Wenceslas

WILLIAM ABINGTON

*William Abington was brought up in Kimbolton, near
Huntingdon, on the edge of the Fens. In this piece he
recalls the pleasure brought by carol singers on a cold, clear
Christmas Eve nearly eighty years ago.*

On 24 December 1913 I was ten years old. The night was
bitterly cold; the tea things had been cleared away and I
relaxed with my book of children's stories. Through the
window a brilliant star stared at me like the tinsel star on top
of the small Christmas tree standing on the piano.

The room had been brightened with sprigs of holly,
mistletoe and ivy. We never bought holly for Christmas, as
just on the other side of the wall surrounding the cemetery at
Newtown was a splendid holly tree. Using the wall as cover
from the prying eyes of the cemetery warden, we cut the best
sprays, and, secreting them under our topcoats, smuggled
them home.

Our parents admonished my brother and me for stealing,
especially from a cemetery, but in that age of innocence we had
no qualms of conscience. The sharp-pointed and scintillating
leaves promise joy and excitement and the ornate red berries
bring back the warmth and good feeling, the sound of carols,
the chiming bells and mirthful laughter.

I felt most comfortable as I sat reading. Mother had just prepared for us a hot supper of large roast potatoes and onions, one of my favourite meals. Suddenly she gave a cry. 'Listen,' and from the direction of the George Hotel corner came the faint sounds of singing and we could just make out the strains of that outstanding carol from Austria, 'Silent Night'.

This carol owes its emergence, so the story goes, to just before Christmas 1818, when mice had eaten through the bellows of the organ in the village church of Oberndorf. The parish priest, Joseph Morh, thought Christmas without music would be unthinkable and he sat down and wrote the simple words of the carol. He asked the organist to compose a tune for them, and when he had done this they sang the song, accompanied on the guitar, that would still be sung centuries later in many churches, proclaimed by many to be the carol of carols.

As we sat listening we knew the next stop of the singers would be outside our house, and father slid down the top window pane so that we could hear them more clearly.

The carol they chose to sing was 'Good King Wenceslas' which honours the patron saint of Czechoslovakia, a monarch killed by his jealous brother, Boleshav, at a chapel door in AD 929. The feast of Stephen which the text reveres is the day after Christmas. We sing it to the tune of an ancient Latin song which John Neale found in a sixteenth century hymnal.

The words had a special appeal to me at that time of the year, for we had meat and sweetmeats at Christmas which we never enjoyed during the rest of the year. We also burned pine logs on the fire and I was actually allowed a sip or two of an innocuous wine on Christmas Day.

As the last verse of the carol died away there came a knock at the door and Walter Ellis, whose deep bass voice was the pride of the choir, held out a small bag. Into it my father dropped a silver coin.

A Christmas Eve Wedding

SYBIL MARSHALL

Fenland Chronicle *is the story of a tough, warm and witty Fenland couple, William Henry and Kate Mary Edwards, compiled by their daughter Sybil Marshall. As she says in her foreword, 'the words and the phrases are those of the old Fen Tiger and his wife who were my parents. They were both magnificent talkers, and fascinated me with their tales of my Huntingdonian forebears from the time when I was wont to be entertained as I rode home on my father's shoulders down a sluddy black fen drove on a cold winter's night, or sat drowsily on the hearthrug with a lap full of kittens before a smouldering, crumbling turf fire and listened as the talk flowed over my head.'* Fenland Chronicle *is divided into 'Dad's Book' and 'Mam's Book'. This account of Will 'En and Kate's Christmas Eve wedding comes from 'Mam's Book'.*

One day when I were twenty-one I walked along the bank to Walton to visit some friends o' my father. When I were coming back, there were Will 'En (or Bill 'Arry, he answered to both) coming along the bank to meet me, and that night he asked me to marry him. He had a beautiful home of his own and enough ready money to buy whatever we wanted to set up a

home with – it were a rare thing, and no mistake, in them days! He bought me a ring the next week, and I went off back to my job at Huntingdon, where I was companion-help to a wonderful old lady. I never told my mother or father – I was afraid of what my father would say, as he was a violent-tempered man.

One Sunday morning Will 'En went to see them, and mother was making some jam tarts. He sat down in father's chair and during the conversation said something about 'when we are married'.

'What did you say?' she said, startled.

'Why, ain't Kate told you we're going to get married come Christmas?' he said.

Mother laid down her rolling pin, and sat down 'all of a heap', in tears. But they were tears of joy, for never had it entered her head that anything so wonderful could have happened as for one of her daughters to catch such a prize like Will 'En. She adored him, and he her, to the very end, and into the bargain he were the only man as couldn't do no wrong

The Anchor Inn and sluice at Upware on a winter's day in the early 1900s

for my father. But things weren't so rosy for him at home, when he told them. His mother didn't want him to marry at all, 'let alone a school-gal' (a reference to my youth compared with him), and his sisters all felt that they were a cut above my family, 'cos they were farmers, and my father only a higgler, with a queer temper, and a curious reputation an' all.

But it di'n't make no difference, and on December 24 we went to St Mary's church in a little trap, with my sister as bridesmaid, and my cousin as best man. My father had one of his awk'ard fits on and wouldn't come to the wedding, so Mother daren't come, and my brother had to give me away.

There weren't no spectators at weddings then, and we had it all to ourselves. We had to pass Will En's father's house on the way, but there was nobody looking out for us there neither. They meant to, it appears, and sent out Bill's sister's little girl, Elsie, who was three, to watch for us. When we got there we could only see Elsie, so we picked her up, just as she was, and took her to church with us; she was the only witness of our wedding except the official party. We stopped at Bill's father's house for tea, and Mother came up in the evening for a little while. We'd cleared the barn, and we kept up the wedding for the best part of the week, dancing and feasting. Bill lost his tie when we were getting ready to go to the church, and never did find it again – he had to wear an old one – the very same thing happened when my sister was married.

We stopped at his father's that night, and about six o'clock the next morning his mother came banging on our door yelling, 'Bill, git up as soon as iver you can – the ole cow's a calving', so although it were Christmas morning and the first morning of our married life into the bargain, he had to get up and be midwife to a cow.

Then after a week we went off to our own home in Lotting Fen.

Hereward's Return

CHARLES MACFARLANE

On a stormy night just before Christmas in the year 1069, local hero Hereward the Wake, back from exile in Flanders and ready to do battle with the Normans, braved the perils of the Wash and sailed into King's Lynn. Next day, Christmas Eve, he travelled by boat, through the fens to Ely, last refuge of the Saxons against the conquering Normans – a voyage that 'no bark had ever made before, and not many have since'. That, at least, is the way Charles Macfarlane tells it in The Camp of Refuge, *a stirring Victorian version of the Hereward story.*

There may be between Thamesis and the Tyne worse seas and more perilous rocks; but when the north-east wind blows right into that gulf, and the waves of the German ocean are driven on by the storms of winter, the practised mariner will tell ye that the navigation of the Wash, the Boston deeps, and the Lynn Deeps, is a fearful thing to those who know the shoals and coasts, and a leap into the jaws of death to those that know them not. Besides the shallows near the shore, there be sandbanks and treacherous shoals in the middle of the bay, and these were oft times shifting their places or changing their shapes.

It was under one of the fiercest and loudest tempests that ever blew from the sky of winter, and upon one of the roughest seas that ever rolled into the Wash, that five barks, which

seemed all to be deeply laden and crowded with men, drove past the shoal called the Dreadful, and made for that other shoal called the Inner Dousing. The sun, which had not been visible the whole day, now showed itself like a ball of fire as it sank in the west behind the flats and fens of Lincolnshire; and when the sun was down the fury of the tempest seemed to increase.

Keeping a little ahead the bark that had first reached the coast glided into Lynn Deeps; and as it advanced towards the mouth of the Ouse, signal-lights or piloting lights rose at every homestead and hamlet. And besides these stationary lights, there were other torches running along the shore close above the line of sea foam. And much was all this friendly care needed, the deeps being narrow and winding and the wind still blowing a hurricane. On this eastern side of the Wash few could have slept, or have tarried in their homes this night; for when – near upon midnight, and as the monks of Lynn were preparing to say matins in the chapel of Saint Nicholas – the five barks swirled safely into the deep and easy bed of the Ouse, and came up to the prior's wharf, let go their anchors and threw their stoutest cordage ashore, the wharf and all the river bank was covered with men, women and children, and the houses in the town behind the river bank were nearly all lighted up, as if it had been Midsummer's eve, instead of the penultimate night of the Novena of Christmas.

The first that landed from the foremost bark was a tall, robust and handsome man, dressed as Saxon noblemen and warriors were wont to dress before the incoming of the ill fashions of Normandie.

He carried in his right hand a long straight and broad sword, the blade of which was curiously sheathed, and the hilt of which formed a cross. When he had crossed the plankings of the wharf, some began to shout, 'It is he! It is Lord Hereward of Brunn! It is Hereward the Saxon! It is the Lord of Brunn,

Lord Hereward of Brunn, as the Victorians saw him

come to get back his own and to help us drive out the Normans.' One Nan of Lynn, a well-famed and well-spoken woman, said as she looked upon the Lord Hereward, 'We Englishwomen of the fens will beat the men-at-arms from Normandie, an we be but led by such a captain as this!'

The person nearest in attendance on Lord Hereward was that lucky wight Elfric, who had been to seek him in foreign parts. He too had more than one tear of joy in his eye as he trod upon the shore; but this tender emotion soon gave way to a hearty if not boisterous mirth, and so he kept shouting, 'Make way for Hereward, the Lord of Brunn!' and kept squeezing the hands of all the men and women and children he knew in Lynn, as they walked towards the convent where Hereward was to rest until daylight.

In the morning, as soon as it was light, Hereward, Elfric and a score of armed men re-embarked in the good ship that had brought them to Lynn, and proceeded up the river Ouse, leaving the other four barks at their moorings under the prior's wharf. Broad and free was the river Ouse, and up as high as the junction of the Stoke, Lord Hereward's bark was favoured by the tide as well as by the wind. Above the Stoke the tide failed; but the wind blew steadily on, and many boats with lusty rowers in them, came down from Ely and Chettisham and Littleport, and took the bark in tow, for the signal-lights and fires which had guided the fleet into Lynn had been carried across the fens and to the Abbey of Ely, and had told my Lord Abbat that the Lord Hereward had come. No bark had ever made such a voyage before, nor have many made it since; but a good while before the sun went down our Lynn mariners made their craft fast to my Lord Abbat's pier, and Hereward and his bold and trusty followers landed in the midst of a throng ten times greater and ten times more jubilant than that which had welcomed them at Lynn.

At the outer gate of the convent Lord Hereward was met

and embraced by Thurstan, the high-hearted abbat of the house, by the archbishop Stigand, the Abbat of Crowland, and by all the prelates and high churchmen; and next by all the cloistered monks of Ely; and next by the lay lords and the Saxon warriors of all parts: and all this right reverend and right noble company shouted, 'Welcome to our chief and our deliverer! Honour and welcome to the young Lord of Brunn!'

As Thurstan led the Saxon hero by the hand towards his own Aula Magna, he said, 'Thou comest at a most suitable moment, and on the verge of the most joyous of all seasons; 'tis the vigil of the Nativity. This Christmas eve, like all good Christians, we feed upon a banquet of eels and fish. At midnight, we have the midnight mass, chanted in our best manner; and tomorrow we feast indeed, and give up all our souls to joy. Tomorrow, then, our bells shall be struck upon so that the Norman knights and men-at-arms shall hear them in Cam-Bridge Castle, and shall tremble while they hear! And our Saxon flags, and the banners of our saints, yea, the great banner of Saint Etheldreda itself, shall be hung out on our walls!'

The young Saxon simply said that he had come back to get back his own, and to help his good countrymen to get back their own; that the Norman yoke was all too grievous to be borne. All were eager to be informed of the strength which the Lord of Brunn brought with him, and of the plans he proposed to pursue. The sum of Hereward's replies was simply this: Elfric had found him out in Flanders, and had delivered him letters which had determined him to quit his adoptive country and return to England. Many English exiles who had been living in the Netherlands had made up their minds to come over with him. Such money as they could command had been applied to the purchase of warlike harness, and to the hiring and equipping of three foreign barks. The master of a bark from Lynn that chanced to be in those parts had offered his bark and the services of himself and his crew for nothing.

· A Fenland Christmas ·

Winter willows and abandoned armour, from Julia Corner's
Hereward the Brave

The gold and silver which my Lord Abbat had sent with
Elfric had been profitably employed; and besides spearheads
and swords, and bows and jackets of mail, the Lynn bark now
lying at my Lord Abbat's pier had brought such a quantity of
Rhenish and Mosel wine as would suffice for the consumption
of the whole house until next Christmas. Counting the men
that had come in all the barks, there were more than one
hundred and ten true-hearted Saxons, well-armed and equip-
ped and well-practised in the use of arms.

It was Lord Hereward's notion that our great house at Ely

and the Camp of Refuge would be best relieved or screened from any chance of attack, by the Saxons making at once a quick and sharp attack all along the Norman lines or posts to the north and north-west of the Isle of Ely. Twenty of the armed men he had brought with him from their wearisome exile, he would leave at Ely; with the rest he would go to the Welland river and make a beginning.

'But thou canst not go yet awhile,' said Abbat Thurstan, thinking of the Christmas festivals and of the Rhenish wines; 'thou canst not quit us, my son, until after the feast of the Epiphany! 'Tis but twelve days from tomorrow, and the Normans are not likely to be a-stirring during those twelve days.'

'True, my Lord Abbat,' said Hereward, 'the Normans will be feasting and rejoicing; but it is on that very account that I must go forthwith in order to take them unprepared and attack their bands separately while they are feasting.'

'Then,' said the abbat, 'thou mayest be back and keep the feast of Epiphany with us.'

Hereward promised he would return if he could. But when he spoke of setting out on the morrow after high mass, not only the Lord Abbat, but everyone that heard him, raised his voice against him, and Hereward yielded to the argument that it would be wicked to begin war on Christmas Day, or to do any manner of thing on that day except praying and feasting.

At this moment the eels and fish of the Christmas-eve supper were all ready, and the best cask of Rhenish which the bark had brought up to my Lord Abbat's pier was broached.

from

Hymn on the Morning of Christ's Nativity

JOHN MILTON

John Milton wrote his earliest poetry in Latin. 'Hymn on the Morning of Christ's Nativity' was his first great poem in English. Full of striking imagery, it was composed in 1629, just after Milton's twenty-first birthday while he was still a student at Christ's College, Cambridge.

It was the Winter wilde,
While the Heav'n-born-childe
All meanly wrapt in the rude manger lies;
Nature in aw to him
Had dofft her gawdy trim,
With her great Master so to sympathize:
It was no season then for her
To wanton with the Sun her lusty Paramour.

But peacefull was the night
Wherein the Prince of light
His raign of peace upon the earth began:

The Windes with wonder whist,
Smoothly the waters kist,
Whispering new joyes to the milde Ocean,
Who now hath quite forgot to rave,
While Birds of Calm sit brooding on the charmed waves,

The Stars with deep amaze
Stand fixt in stedfast gaze,
Bending one way their pretious influence,
And will not take their flight,
For all the morning light,
Or Lucifer that often warn'd them thence;
But in their glimmering Orbs did glow,
Untill their Lord himself bespake, and bid them go.

Dad's Christmas

LINDSAY WILLIAMSON

A printer by profession, Lindsay Williamson has been fascinated by Fenland folklore since he wrote a school project on Hereward the Wake as a lad. Since then he has produced several collections of stories and poems including Fen Folk *and* Tales They Tell. *His father was brought up near Boston in the Lincolnshire Fens. When, in 1989, the family got together for Christmas as usual, Lindsay had his notebook handy.*

· A Fenland Christmas ·

Many strange and unaccountable things my father claims to have seen out in the fens: ghostly green lights flickering across the marshes at dead of night, black-hooded figures standing by an old stone barn, and once, when the family had moved to Bourne, he swears he was prevented from walking under a falling tree by a mysterious, invisible hand pulling at his shoulder.

But today, as is traditional on Christmas Day, with the family gathered round the fireside he has gentler tales to tell — tales of Christmas when he was a boy growing up on a remote farm near Boston. The yearly ritual never loses its appeal, and as the stories unfold it is possible to detect a childish light in his eyes as the old memories spin back some sixty years or more:

Well, as you all know, [he says] we had a largish farm out near Sibsey. Grandad and Grandma Garwell owned the farm, and my Dad, your Grandad [he nodded at my sister and me], was the local blacksmith.

We always had plenty of games to play and if we got fed up we could always go and watch Dad shoeing. The smell from a hot shoe applied to a raw hoof became one of my favourites. I only have to think about it now to see Dad disappearing behind a thick cloud of pungent steam!

Mum loved Christmas — she became like a child herself as the great day approached. Throughout the year we would collect all the little scraps of coloured paper that came our way and use them to make paper chains. On Christmas Eve we stuck them in loops across the room. Then the tree — always huge, or so it seems looking back — was brought in and decorated with real candles. I can remember the tin holders that clipped around the branches as if it were only yesterday.

Before going to bed on Christmas Eve we all went out to

the stables and gave Beauty and Blossom, our two shire horses, their mince pies. I loved that moment. The stables would be full of mellow lantern light whilst the two 'gentle giants' as we called them, ate the pies from our open palms. I remember how their noses tickled!

Mum always told us we had to leave before midnight because that's when Beauty and Blossom would go down on their knees in honour of Christmas morning. I always liked that story and often wanted to sneak back out of the house to see if it were true. I never did of course. I suppose I always wanted to believe it.

Before going to bed we hung up our pillow cases on either side of the fireplace and left Santa his customary mince pie and glass of sherry. I'm sure Dad enjoyed that bit

'Many strange and unaccountable things my father claims to have seen out in the fens'

of Christmas! In the morning we would get up early and open our presents. I think it must have been 1928 when I got my Meccano set. Boy, was I proud of that! I was able to join pieces of metal together just like Dad.

Later we'd help Dad with feeding and watering the horses and Mum with preparing the goose. Church was too far away to attend but we were able to listen to carols on the 'cat's whisker' later in the day. What a sight we must have been – all sitting round the big table handing the headset on to the next person after we had had our allotted time.

Sometimes we used to get Blossom or Beauty out and trot along with the cart to visit neighbours. But more often than not we would stay in and play games like snakes and ladders or 'pin the tail on the donkey'.

That was a funny game! A cartoon picture of a donkey minus his tail was stuck on the wall and we'd all take turns, blindfold, trying to pin his tail in the right place on the picture. I remember Dad once losing his bearings completely and ending up sticking the tail into the opposite wall! Laugh! We thought we'd never stop!

Mum was a great one for practical jokes. I remember one year we sat down to Christmas tea and suddenly I saw my plate give a little jump. Then another one. I couldn't believe it – an ordinary plate sitting on an ordinary table yet every so often it gave a little jump. I looked at Mum and I looked at the plate. It took me a long time to work out that she'd rigged a rubber pipe under the cloth that swelled whenever she pressed the bulb at her end!

Ah, they were good times and no mistake. Now, who's got the walnuts?

A Victorian Christmas

JOHN DURRANT

Contemporary critics of the commercial abuse of Christmas deplore the corruption of a religious festival. Expressions of nostalgia for the values of a less materialistic age are often heard. Such sentiments, however, are not peculiar to the modern age. In 1881, for instance, one contributor to the *Cambridge Chronicle* wrote of Christmas as 'above all, the season when so many yield to noxious drinking and many move to noxious and expensive gluttony'. The rival *Cambridge Express* printed a 'Rhyme for the Time' which apparently expressed an eternal theme:

> Christmas comes but once a year
> That plea's supposed to be a softener
> But since it costs one precious dear
> One's precious glad it don't come oftener!

Perhaps, then, it is worth looking more closely, through the pages of local newspapers, at the nature and experience of a Victorian Christmas over a hundred years ago.

Christmas Day 1881 fell on a Sunday and, with Monday as the Boxing Day bank holiday, many people had an unusual three-day break. The Early Closing Society duly issued a notice

to the effect that, 'The Principal Establishments in the town will be closed on Monday and Tuesday, December 26th and 27th.'

For those in the retail and food trades, December was obviously a busy period. The *Express* reported that the stationers, clothiers, jewellers and flower-sellers had put on an admirable display of seasonal wares. At Alexandra House in Petty Cury S. Ballard organized his annual Christmas bazaar. The advertisements advised clients to come early as the goods were mainly of foreign manufacture and could not be repeated.

The *Chronicle* stated that on the Wednesday night prior to Christmas the streets were crowded with prospective buyers and, in common with the other papers, gave a detailed account of each butcher's merchandise.

Roast beef was the traditional Christmas fare, as the poultry shows were not held until the following January. However, there was some controversy over the importation of American provisions and one group of butchers went so far as to advertise their produce under the headline, 'No American meat sold'.

Church and charity were an integral part of the Victorian Christmas festival though newspaper reports of the religious services pay more attention to the floral arrangements and use of Christian maxims than the spiritual message. There was only one account of a sermon, in contrast to the long and detailed descriptions of decorations in eighteen parish churches which both the *Chronicle* and the *Express* carried.

One item did, however, mar the comfortable and uncontroversial representation of religious celebrations. In a letter to the *Chronicle*, a churchgoer at Ely objected to the 'indecent haste with which officials proceed to lock up the brazen gates of the choir immediately after divine service is over lest perchance any poor man or woman should intrude among those who are able to pay a fee for seeing the inner glories of the church'. The writer went on to comment that it was not

the poor who talked noisily and behaved irreverently in church.

If the eighteenth century could be said to be the age of 'conspicuous consumption', then the nineteenth century was the age of conspicuous charity. The pages of the Cambridge papers were strewn with items of private and institutional philanthropy.

The charitable sources, the method of distribution and the content were haphazard and varied. The Ragged Sunday School Dorcas Society, for instance, provided children with clothing at only one third of the real cost. Through the office of the *Town Crier* St Peter's College distributed eighty bushels of coal to the poor. The executors of Cook's Charity doled out bread and coal to the widows of the parish of St Andrew the Great. The Mayoress, Mrs Death, continued her annual custom and gave one hundred parcels to the poor who lived in the King Street area.

Throughout the county the gentry and clergy discharged

King's Parade, Cambridge, in the 1880s

· A Fenland Christmas ·

what they considered to be their social duty. At West Wickham Mr de Fraine gave to all the widows and elderly persons one hundredweight of coal, a pound of sugar, a quarter pound of tea and one shilling. The labourers also received quantities of tea, sugar and coal.

Despite the commendable intentions of many of the donors, it was indicative of Victorian society that charity was an essential part of the domestic economy, not only of disadvantaged groups such as the elderly, the unemployed and widows, but even those in employment. Low income groups, especially the labouring classes, looked upon charity as a necessary provider of minor luxuries if not necessities.

For the inmates of the workhouses, Christmas Day meant a departure from the dull and stifling routine. At the Cambridge Union Workhouse (afterwards the Maternity Hospital), children began the day singing carols to an audience which included some of the guardians and Sunday visitors.

According to the *Chronicle*, decorations of a very appropriate kind had been arranged in all parts of the building. The festive arrangements were 'remarkably well-ordered due to the good management of master and matron, despite the ill-constructed nature of the whole building'.

The 239 inmates sat down to a Christmas dinner of '250 lbs of roast beef, six bushels of potatoes and 250 lbs of plum pudding':

Old and young were served in a most ample manner, and it was indeed a pleasing sight to watch the magical disappearance of the viands. . . . No doubt in these days of reform there are many things in our Poor Law which would be all the better for a little alteration, but not the way in which Christmas Day is observed in our Unions. For on that day the most abundant good cheer, geniality and non-officialdom prevails.

· A Fenland Christmas ·

Like the *Chronicle*, the *Express* had nought but praise for the workhouse Christmas:

> It would have done the immortal Dickens and Cruikshank a power of good could they have strolled through the various wards . . . to find Bumble a thing of the past and the young and old Olivers with such a sufficiency that the need to present their basins again was entirely removed.

Similar festive scenes were reported at the Chesterton Union Workhouse, but apparently any traditional decoration was absent. At a meeting of the guardians it was noted that, 'Miss Boucher had asked permission to give the children a Christmas tree on the 4th of January'.

One dissident from the general acclaim of the munificence of the workhouse Christmas contributed a 'seasonable suggestion' to both the *Chronicle* and the *Express*. He claimed that 'children could be fed amply and well without flesh meat' and recommended the use of a vegetarian cookbook. He went on to cite the example of the Manchester authorities who, the previous Christmas, 'fed 500 children with good soup and plum pudding at the cost of only 2½d per child'.

As a concession to the Christmas holiday the newspapers devoted space to the amusement and edification of their readers. There were festive poems and short stories, a review of Christmas card designs and assorted jokes, puzzles and 'golden thoughts'. Included among the latter was a contentious maxim, reputedly of Chinese origin:

> We require four things of woman. That virtue dwell in her heart; that modesty play on her brow; that sweetness flow from her lips; that industry occupy her hand.

Ode by a Christmas Pudding at Sea

ARTHUR LOCKER

This cheerful ode is an example of the kind of festive poems that appeared in Fenland newspapers at Christmas in Victorian times.

To all you puddings now on shore
I write to give a notion
Of what mishaps there are in store
For puddings born on Ocean;
It blew a gale from sou'sou'west,
But the skipper's wife she did her best.
As she kneaded the dough on her own sea chest,
With a fal lal lal lal la.

The vessel gave a lurch, a wave
Right down the hatchway came;
The skipper's wife stood stout and brave,
I wish I'd done the same;
For I rolled in a fright along the floor,
And the skipper coming in at the door,
Gave me a kick, which my jacket tore,
With a fal lal lal lal la.

· *A Fenland Christmas* ·

His good wife gathered up the bits,
And put my limbs together;
Says she, 'I must have lost my wits
To cook in such foul weather;
But sailor boys they love good cheer,
And Christmas comes but once a year,
So I won't be beat, I'll persevere.'
With a fal lal lal lal la.

The galley fire burnt bright and clear
As she put me in the pot;
Thinks I, 'It suits me being here,
I feel so jolly hot.'
But a great green sea burst over the deck,
And I fancied myself a perfect wreck,
In cold salt water up to my neck,
With a fal lal lal lal la.

Cries cook, 'The pudding's surely spoiled.'
'No, no!' says the skipper's wife;
'That Christmas pudding shall be boiled,
If I sacrifice my life.'
With her own fair hands she lit the fire,
And though the waves rose higher and higher,
At last she accomplished her desire,
With a fal lal lal lal la.

And here they are, these sailor boys,
All full of mirth and glee;
They sit in a ring with lots of noise,
And they're going to eat poor Me!
When smash! there comes a roaring squall,
A lurch – and into the scuppers fall
Sailor boys, Christmas pudding and all,
With a fal lal lal lal la.

'Welcome to the Poor of Walsoken'

Christmas was always a busy time for the Rector of Walsoken, the Revd John Young, Chairman of the Wisbech Board of Guardians. In 1889, for instance, he spent Christmas Day at the Wisbech Union Workhouse, helping serve Christmas dinner, carving one of the largest joints. After the 'inmates' had eaten their fill he could not resist reminding them that, 'though they were in the Workhouse, they were better off than thousands of people in large towns to whom such a thing as a Christmas dinner was unknown'. He had visited many workhouses, he said, but knew of none 'in which the comfort of the inmates was as much studied as at Wisbech where the Guardians, unlike those of a certain district of Cheshire, did not grudge them the use of knives and forks'. Two days later he was again carving roast beef, this time for the poor of Walsoken. The Wisbech Standard *reports.*

Friday, Dec. 27th 1889 will long be remembered as a red-letter day by the poor of Walsoken, and with gratitude as well. It is evident that the Rector of the parish (the Rev. J. Young) cares for the temporal as well as the spiritual welfare of his parishioners not only as Chairman of the Board of Guardians over which he so ably presides, but also in other ways, not the least of which being the activity and energy with

which he arranges and carries out the annual Christmas entertainment to the aged and needy of his parish. Bloomfield's lines,

> Old winter comes on with a frown,
> A terrible frown for the poor,
> In a season so rude and forlorn;
> How can age, how can fancy bear
> The silent neglect and the scorn
> Of those who have plenty to spare.

hardly apply to the parish of Walsoken (though they have but too apt a significance in several other places in the Fen and Marshland Districts) and may it always be so.

Upwards of 300 persons of all ages sat down to an excellent and substantial dinner followed by a capital tea and an entertainment. It is hardly to be supposed that the Rector could have defrayed the entire expense out of his own pocket, although he was a liberal (in its true sense) contributor to the fund. The other subscribers included the worthy representative of North West Norfolk, Lord Henry Bentinck, MP, who also contributed very liberally, and Mr R. Bath, whose generous donation was an example to be followed by other members of the great 'Radical' party, whose names never appear by any chance in subscription lists despite their blatant assertions that they are 'friends' of the working man.

The treat as usual took place in the New Walsoken Ward Schools, the several rooms being prettily decorated with evergreens, texts etc, whilst the entrance gateway was surmounted by an arch of evergreens of the 'triumphal' rather than 'ecclesiastical' character, which bore the device 'Welcome to the Poor of Walsoken' in large letters.

Dinner was served shortly after one o' clock. The Rev. Young and Mrs Young were assisted by a number of willing

helpers who carved and otherwise attended to the needs of the guests. The bill of fare included three heavy rounds of beef, some prime legs of mutton, both roasted and boiled, several kinds of vegetables and some excellent plum puddings. Grace having been said, every justice was done to the good things provided, and after the tables had been cleared, a move was made for the well-heated classrooms, where a very pleasant time was spent till tea was ready.

After tea there was another interval followed by a pleasant evening's entertainment. Local butcher, Mr J.S. Johnson of the Market Place, Wisbech, sang several of his well-known character songs, some of which were accompanied by the banjo, in splendid style, eliciting hearty encores, his best efforts probably being 'The Only Girl I Love', 'Wedding Bells' and the 'Awful Little Scrub'. The Wisbech Union Minstrel Troupe (consisting of the Workhouse boys) under the direction of the industrial trainer, Mr Goodley Fisher, came upon the platform three or four times and gave some very amusing sketches in a manner which reflected much credit upon Mr Fisher's instruction. Among the most attractive items in the programme were two duets by Mr B.W. Pywell and Miss Munson, 'Country Courtship' and 'Pretty Polly Hopkins', which piece being loudly encored, whilst Mr H. Edwards of Wisbech gave an excellent stump oration upon the Temperance Question.

Mrs W.W. Green of Walsoken sang some very pretty ballads in grand style, eliciting hearty applause. Nor must we forget the Walsoken handbell ringers who contributed selections in their well-known good style.

At the end of the programme came a hearty vote of thanks. The Rev. Young replied that during the eighteen years he had been rector of the parish it had always been his aim to do all he could to promote the welfare of all classes especially the poor. He was pleased to find they had all enjoyed themselves so

much and trusted that the gathering would not be the last of its kind which would be held in Walsoken.

We must also state that several of those present were inmates of the Wisbech Union Workhouse belonging to Walsoken parish. There was no one forgotten, not even the sick poor, who were unable to be present, and whose Christmas dinners were forwarded to them. May the clergy and people of other parishes go and do likewise.

A Sober Christmas in King's Lynn

In 1889 the poor people of the Wisbech district were able to enjoy a festive Christmas. Fifty years earlier, conditions for the needy were much grimmer. The 1834 Report of the Royal Commission on the Poor Law had led to the building of the Union workhouses throughout the country during the 1830s. Three Poor Law Commissioners were responsible for deciding policy on 'poor relief'. This 1840s newspaper report on Christmas in King's Lynn suggests, however, that the edicts of these 'Three Kings of Somerset House' did not always meet with local approval.

The season of Christmas has been celebrated in the town and neighbourhood of King's Lynn by friendly meetings and

· A Fenland Christmas ·

The Custom House, King's Lynn, around 1900

festive hilarity. With the weather seasonable, cheerful and healthy, all conspired to welcome in Christmas – 'the joyous period of the year'.

There may indeed have been reports that some teetotallers have, during this jovial season, forgotten their 'pledge', and swerved considerably from 'total abstinence'. However, if they never do worse than make a little merry at this jocund period of the year, which for ages has been the season of festivity and rejoicing, we hope they will not be very culpable. Extremes are liable to produce their opposites, and total abstinence may produce a reaction towards excess, just as immoderate intemperance has induced some to become dedicated teetotallers and total abstinence devotees.

On Christmas Day the inmates of the King's Lynn Union Workhouse were treated with plum pudding and an extra allowance of meat for dinner, and in the afternoon and evening the men had pipes and tobacco and the women and children were regaled with tea.

Should the Three Kings of Somerset House hear of this, we fear they will be highly offended at this disobedience to their high behests! For, if we recollect aright, all Christmas indulgences of this kind were strictly forbidden by their humane mightinesses – the Poor Law Commissioners.

College Feasting

REVD H.I.C. BLAKE

Most of the students having gone home, Christmas festivities in Cambridge colleges in the last century were generally for the benefit of Fellows. Not allowed to marry until 1882, Fellows in those days usually lived in their colleges for much of the year. Some colleges were especially noted for their sumptuous Christmas fare. St John's, for instance, where Fellows and guests traditionally feasted on an enormous 'Christmas pie'. Or Sidney Sussex, where the Revd H.I.C. Blake, one-time Fellow of King's College, was invited to dine.

The winter season brings with it much of sociality in the various colleges, when most of the young men are gone to their respective homes (the reins of discipline being much relaxed). I allude to the joyous and festive time of Christmas.

In some colleges, such as St John's and Sidney, as applies equally to some at Oxford, the boar's head graces the table, and the wassail cup takes its round on the supper table. I recollect being invited to partake of the Christmas festivities at Sidney, where, as usual, the boar's head with his gilded teeth, and a famous supply of brawn, were the admiration of the guests. By the way, at this said college of Sidney, Oliver Cromwell was a student, and an oaken table is shown as having belonged to him.

The strictness of the collegiate rules were at this time

· A Fenland Christmas ·

Garrett Hostel Bridge over the River Cam on a frosty winter's
day in the 1890s

dispensed with; and a young man, a very fresh man indeed
from the land of the taters, was among the invited guests, he
having considered it, and justly too, not worth the while at
that cold season of the year to return to the north of Ireland for
so short a time as the Christmas holidays.

He had played his part very well with the knife and fork and
he thought he might as well wind it up with the orange,
which had been inserted in the boar's mouth, by way of
ornament. No sooner thought of than done, but instead of
extricating the orange only from its recess, one of the gilded
grinders accompanied it; nevertheless he very soon demolished
the orange, redolent of boar, but completed the action by
pocketing the extracted tooth.

I should not have envied him his feelings at the time when
he caught the eye of the master, who was too much of the

gentlemanly host to make any remark at the time before strangers, or spoil the conviviality of the meeting. I have no doubt that in the morning he had somewhat of an admonitory lecture, with an intimation that such actions were not fitting to gentlemen of that college.

An Icy Road to Ely

REVD H.I.C. BLAKE

A hard Fenland winter always meant good skating and 1814 was just such a winter. Being an indifferent skater didn't stop the Reverend Blake proposing to skate from Cambridge to Ely for a bet. In The Cantab, or a Few Adventures and Misadventures in After Life *he tells the story.*

In the hard winter of 1814, the sluggish Cam, whose current is scarcely ever perceptible, became one beautiful sheet of ice, and was bearable all the way down to Ely. It was a strange sight to view the skaiters, many of them in their caps and gowns, cutting figures on their steel propellers, whirling away under Clare Hall, Gerard's Hostel and Trinity Bridges, their gowns streaming behind them; while others, young beginners, were cutting very awkward figures, to the no small amusement of bystanders and senior fellows, who, perhaps, would have

thought it a little infra dig to have mingled with the young men, and whose limbs were not quite so pliant.

I was but a very indifferent skaiter, owing to being a little weak in the ankles at that time; still I could manage to get on tolerably well, and keep my head from coming into contact with the ice. One afternoon, as we were sitting in the Combination Room, the subject of skaiting was broached, and that it was now possible to go down to Ely on the ice. Out of bravado, I suppose, I said that for a good wager to make it worth my while I would skait to Ely. All the Fellows knew that I was a poor performer, and, consequently, I was soon accommodated with bets to my mind. The terms were, that I was to go on my skaits on the ice as I could in three hours to Ely; to be allowed one hour there for refreshment, and to

Schoolboys playing in the snow outside the King's School, Ely, 1900

return on foot by land to Cambridge in four hours; and that I was actually to skait by myself from the Sluice on Jesus Common to Chesterton without any assistance.

It was considered almost a certainty that I should never reach that spot. I began to think that I had made a foolish bet; but still a something urged me to proceed. I started at ten from the Sluice, two splendid skaiters of our College volunteering to go with me to Ely, if requisite, to see if the feat was performed. I made sad work of it down to Chesterton, two miles, taking me a full half an hour to do that. The distance to Ely is twenty miles by water. Now, then, I called to my aid my noble dog, Nelson, whom I had brought with me with his collar on, and, having run a rope through a ring on his collar, and with a loop at the other end, I told him to 'go on', and, by keeping my body a little bent, and my feet close together, he drew me in a rapid style.

I soon passed my two overlookers, who called on me to stop for them. 'No, no,' says I, 'Go on, Nelson,' and before I had gone half the way en route to Ely I had lost sight of them. It was awful work, going at the rate I did; the ice bent in so many places, particularly in turns of the river, where the wind had exerted its power, and kept it from freezing so soon as on the other parts, and in the very deep places it looked dismally black. I kept a good hold of the rope, looking out for a squall, for I knew that if the ice had broken I had a life preserver in old Nelson.

To make short of the matter, I reached Ely in two hours and a half exactly. Proceeding to the Lamb Inn, I ordered mutton chops for two. The cloth was soon laid, and the waiter, making his appearance, asked if another gentleman was coming to dine with me. I told him he was already arrived. After helping myself to a chop, and the old dog at the same time, share and share alike, to the no small surprise of the waiter, telling him that I thought he equally deserved his

dinner as myself, as he had earned me ten guineas. Just as the clock was striking one, in came my two watchmen, pretty well tired. I staid at Ely until two, the time fixed, and then started to run back to Cambridge. They said they would give me an hour's law before they started on their return in a post chaise. They overtook me at Milton, four miles from Cambridge, and we all went into College together, and proceeding to the Combination Room, took the party there assembled all aback on finding that I had accomplished my task. The money was paid, and I was the Lion of the evening.

Skating on Whittlesey Mere

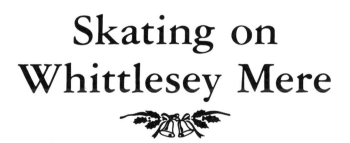

The Fens used to produce some of the finest speed skaters in the country, with local matches generally drawing large crowds. According to this newspaper report, over six thousand people gathered on Whittlesey Mere on the Monday after Christmas in 1840, both to skate themselves and to watch sixteen of the best runners of the day compete for prize money of £10. The skaters raced in pairs, the winners of each round going on to the next.

On Monday last, agreeably to public notice, a match for £10 came off here, open to all comers; and as the notice was given

some days beforehand, and had been extensively circulated, a competition between the best runners of the day was fully expected and as satisfactorily realized. The sum run for was liberally subscribed by several gentlemen residing in the vicinity of the Mere.

The ice was of the best description, and from the stillness of the wind during the frost, the whole extent of near 1000 acres of water was frozen over without a single wake – smooth and shining as a mirror; and as a skating arena, certainly not to be surpassed (if equalled) in the United Kingdom. About ten o'clock the various drains and dykes leading to the Mere in all directions were crowded with skaters, all verging to the centre of attraction; and by the time the first race began it was calculated that from 6,000 to 7,000 persons were at the time on the Mere.

A skating race on Whittlesey Mere, from the *Illustrated London News*, 1850

Numerous men in clusters, moved about, traversing large distances with the celerity of a steam-engine – now stopping, and then scudding away in the opposite direction. Of course the order of the day was running, not figuring; one or two gentlemen in the latter branch attracted a little attention and some pity that they should waste their time wheeling in circles of three yards diameter, instead of pursuing their onward and exhilarating course on the pinions of the wind.

For the race there were sixteen competitors. The course, half a mile in length, was tastefully marked out by laurels placed in earth on the ice, the two ends having much larger pieces than the intervening ones. The course was traversed twice, consequently two miles was the running distance of each race.

At twelve o' clock the first round commenced. The eight winners then contended and Needham, Tomblin, Sharman and Searle were successful. In the contest between these four, Tomblin and Sharman were victorious. The race between Tomblin and Needham was well-contested, and it is but justice to add that Needham, in the middle of the race, had to adjust his skates, or the contest might have been much nearer, or the result different.

Some time elapsed before the start of the final race between Tomblin and Sharman; and expectation was at its highest to witness the contest between the best men of the day; but after the start there was little doubt as to the ultimate success of Tomblin, as he was first throughout and came in easily some yards ahead. A mile in the last and several of the other races was done in $3\frac{1}{2}$ minutes, which allowing for time occupied in turning must be considered excellent running.

At the conclusion and as soon as the result was known, which was after four o'clock, the parties left the Mere in scores, and at the fastest pace they were masters of; so that the Mere, which had been thronged all day, was in less than half an hour quite deserted. We are happy to say that no serious accident

Sports on Whittlesey Mere in the 1860s

occurred, but there were plenty of damaged noses and darkened eyes in consequence of fouling or the skaters running into each other.

Many expressed regret that, as notice had been given for draining the Mere and adjoining lands, this was the last season in all probability they should skate on its waters; but as everything else is improving, why should Whittlesey Mere be exempted, for the pleasures of boating and skating, when it will, if drained, yield a respectable living to many families and employment to hundreds.

The Fen Skaters of Welney Wash

FRANCES COLLINGWOOD

To the little village of Welney belongs the honour of having bred some of the fastest speed skaters of all time – men like William ('Turkey') Smart; George ('Fish'), his nephew; George's younger brother James; William ('Gutta Percha') See, and his son George. All of them learned their art upon that stretch of swampy land known as Welney Wash, which so often froze over in winter. In the 1890s they were destined to spread the fame of Fenland skaters as far afield as Norway and Holland.

Those were the days when English winters lived up to their name and produced enough ice each year to last sufficiently long for the people of the Fens to acquire great skill in the old English pastime of speed skating. For this form of sport was very popular in this country long before the more genteel art of figure skating became the fashion. Cambridgeshire indeed proved an ideal nursery for skaters by virtue of its long stretches of ice.

It must have been an exhilarating sight to watch the country folk, in the days before roads were reasonably passable, flying over the ice at a speed of between nine and ten miles an hour, as they went about their business. Village was linked with village in this manner, and the Fen skaters were said to be able

to cover forty to seventy miles in a day with the utmost enjoyment.

Nowhere else in England so closely resembles the Dutch countryside, and the similarity has bred a keen sense of affinity between the two countries. Ice skating may be considered the natural sport of Holland, and the inhabitants of so small a village as Welney were given the status of international ambassadors in the days when the peasantry of one country rarely came into contact with that of another. Plain, honest, country folk like the Smarts would go sailing off to Friesland to try their luck in skating contests with the Dutch, and on occasions they even travelled as far as Norway to take part in international competitions.

Of the three famous Smarts of Welney, the name of 'Turkey' stands supreme. He skated into the limelight in the year of 1854, after defeating Larmen Regester, another Fen champion, and remained unbeatable for almost a decade. His most formidable rival was another native of Welney, the remarkable 'Gutta Percha' See, but it was not until 1867, when 'Turkey' had attained the sere and yellow age of forty, that 'Gutta Percha' succeeded in beating him.

In 1878 'Turkey''s nephew, young George 'Fish' Smart, brought fresh laurels to the family name by becoming champion skater of England. He appears to have been in a class to himself as far as style was concerned, and caused quite a sensation in the world of speed skating. During the winter 1879/80 he actually skated in twenty-seven races without a single defeat; and the following season he broke his own record by gaining a further series of twenty-eight victories. Not until 1889, when he was over thirty years of age, was the championship wrested from him, and the fact that he was beaten by his own younger brother, James, must have made defeat almost as sweet as victory.

The race on 18 December 1878, in which young 'Fish'

Old-style skating champions, 'Turkey' Smart and 'Gutta Percha' See, at Littleport in 1895

Smart caused such a sensation by outskating the champions of his day, must have remained a lively topic for discussion for many a winter afterwards. It was run at Mepal, for a prize of £10, and sixteen of England's fastest skaters competed. But it was the champions of Welney who swept all before them. 'Turkey' Smart and 'Gutta Percha' See won their respective heats, and were pitted against one another in the second heat. It proved a close and exciting race, which 'Gutta Percha' just managed to pull off. In the third heat he was drawn to skate against young 'Fish'. Amidst tumultuous excitement the younger man passed the winning post first. The final was fought out between the two young Georges, 'Fish', the nephew of 'Turkey' Smart, and 'Gutta Percha's' son, who doesn't appear to have had a nickname. 'Fish' won easily and so entered upon the successful career which was to last until 1889.

James has always been considered to be the smartest Smart of them all. Not content with beating the local champions, he crossed oceans and seas in search of bigger and better laurels. In 1890 he won the mile race at Lingay Fen in 3 minutes 8 seconds, which is very nearly twenty miles an hour. The following year he travelled to Norway, where he beat all comers in a five mile race, his time being 15 minutes $19\frac{2}{5}$ seconds.

In 1892 he was back in Norway to win the mile in 2 minutes 53 seconds, the improved time on his 1890 performance being probably due to the superiority of the Norwegian ice. James also took part in international contests in Friesland, where he carried off many a prize.

Those were the days when every champion skated for his own honour and glory, as well as that of his country. Representative teams, such as now take part in the Olympic Games, were unknown when the Smarts reigned at Welney. These doughty champions paid their own travelling expenses, and banked upon prize money to keep them in pocket.

What fine enterprising fellows they were, and how proud the people of the Fens must have felt of their exploits! Do descendants of the Smart and See families still reside at Welney, I wonder? If so, are they able to uphold the skating traditions of their famous forebears?

The Duddleston Cup

C. WOODE

1895 was the best winter skaters had known for many a year with twelve solid weeks of frost. On 11 January the first fixture of the season, the Duddleston Cup, was held at Littleport. Mr Duddleston of Chicago, a native of Wisbech, had only recently presented the cup, won the year before by international champion, J.C. Aveling of March. Though not fully fit after a bad fall in Stockholm during the World Championships, Aveling competed again in 1895. Woode's poem tells the story.

Ho! Listen gallant gentlemen,
Ho! Lend a kindly ear;
To how a gallant race was run
Full early in the year:

· A Fenland Christmas ·

To how the Cup of Duddleston
Was fought for and was won,
And how the people raised a roar
To see the way they scratched and tore
Before the deed was done!

Oh, every Fenman far and near
To see the race was fain:
And crowds that day to Littleport
Kept pouring in by train.
From London town and countryside,
From Cambridge and from Lynn;
From Spalding, March, and all the Fen
In hundreds – women – children – men
That day were pouring in!

There, fathers with their children,
And husbands with their wives,
And lovers with their sweethearts gay
Were skating for their lives.
And greybeards from the Fenland
The deeds of heroes sung,
And told how they had done the mile
In record time – without a smile
They told it to the young.

Big was the race of Duddleston,
A trophy rare to win;
And fourteen names of some renown
That day were handed in –
One Palmer of Prickwillow,
And Aveling, the fast;
That Aveling who held the cup,
Nor thought that day to give it up –
Though destined to be past!

· A Fenland Christmas ·

And Tebbit came from Milton,
A 'skating' name he bore;
And Little hailed from Littleport
(A port without a shore!)
And Flanders, known throughout the Fen
A skater fast and strong;
And Ward, and Crisp, and other men,
E. Shepperson and speedy 'Ben',
That day had 'come along!'

And now against each other
With might and main they vie;
And Palmer soon had shot his belt
And Anderton his die;
And then, alas, did Aveling,
Not fit to run the race,
Right manfully essay to run
To keep the Cup that he had won,
And hold the premier place.

And thousands watched the contest,
And thousands raised a cheer,
To see how pluckily he stuck
The hero of last year.
And thousands yelled for Tebbit,
Right glad to see him first;
And round the winning post and course
His friends had cheered till they were hoarse,
To see his final burst!

But still the Cup of Duddleston
No man might call his own,
For Flanders, Tebbit, Ward and Thorpe
All had their eyes on home!

The final heat of a skating match at Littleport in 1890
between J. Smart and T. Wells

And men said to each other
How everyone had heard:
How Ward and Thorpe had showed their speed,
How Tebbit almost flew – at need,
And Flanders – like a bird.

And Ward ran hard his rival
The envied prize to earn,
And pressing on him all the way
He beat him at the turn.
And none were left but Tebbit,
And Thorpe by Brampton sent,
And what a cheer went round the ring
To see them fly as on the wing,
Their high ambition lent.

Like arrow from the bow-string,
Like lightning from the cloud,

· A Fenland Christmas ·

When Heaven's artillery flashes far,
And thunder crashes loud!
Like two twin-flying thunderbolts
They speed them on their way,
And side by side, and stride by stride,
Like phantoms of the night they glide,
Or heralds of the day!

From all that eager multitude
Scarce did a sound arise,
They watched the fortunes of the race
With all devouring eyes:
But in the straight for victory
They shouted with one mind;
When Tebbit came down like a flash,
With endless pluck and endless dash –
And Ben was just behind!

And so the Cup of Duddleston
And medal all of gold,
The honour and the premier place
This year shall Tebbit hold!
And Duddleston – Chicago –
Will hear the news with joy,
To see his trophy won by men
Who lived and skated on the Fen,
Where he was man and boy!

And that is how, gay gentlemen!
The cup was won this year,
And that is how the Fenmen strive
Such goodly spoils to bear!
To sign themselves 'The Champion',
To win the envied prize,

Admiring cheers from all the crowd,
The welcomes and the plaudits loud,
And smiles from lovely eyes!

Yet some are all for Hendon,
Welsh Harp or Lingay Fen;
And some prefer the oval track,
Amongst our skating men:
But those who run at Littleport
They love the good old style,
In all good faith and sportsman's love
They run the course as that above,
With three turns to the mile!

A Sermon on Skating

W.H. BARRETT

An original slant on skating is given by W.H. Barrett,
who lived at Brandon Creek, a tiny hamlet north of Ely.
Most of his Fen tales he heard told on Saturday nights at
his local, the Ship Inn. According to Enid Porter, who
edited Tales from the Fens, *this sermon was delivered by*

· *A Fenland Christmas* ·

a lay preacher, Rhiny Fletcher, in 1900 in the Steam Engine Primitive Methodist Chapel on the Hundred Foot River.

Now all of you knew me when I spent my Sundays skating instead of preaching, but that was when I worked for the old Devil. But I gave him notice and now I work for another Master, though that doesn't go to say I never go skating. What I want to tell you is this: that the first skater we read about is Job. Who was Job? Well, I'll tell you. He was a Fenman. You want to know how I know that? It's in the book he wrote, thousands of years ago, where he says: 'Behemoth lieth in covert reed and fen.'

I don't know who Behemoth was, he might have been a gamekeeper or something like that, but what I do know is, that there's reed and there's fen, and if Job hadn't lived in the Fens, how would he have known about reeds and fen?

Now you want to know how I know that Job was a skater. Well, doesn't he say: 'By the breath of God frost is given?' And you know, as well as I do, frost makes ice and ice makes skating. And if Job hadn't been a skater he wouldn't have written: 'My days are swifter than a weaver's shuttle.' What he wanted us to know was that he skated backwards and forwards like you do today, only I'm not going to say he was like you, skating from one pub to the next along the river.

There's something else too, to show I'm right. Look at my face; all you can see is wrinkles, and if you want to know what caused those wrinkles, it was skating into the sun with my eyes half-shut. And Job did the same. Listen: 'And Thou hast filled me with wrinkles.' That's good enough for me. But if you want to hear more, then he writes: 'The face of the deep is frozen.' What he means by that is: 'Get out your pattens, the ice will bear you.' And he goes on to say: 'The waters are hid as with a stone.' If he stood here today, instead of me, you'd hear

· A Fenland Christmas ·

Fun on frozen washes at Upware in the 1920s — Archie
Housden is pulling local midwife Louisa Stevens

him telling you the ice would bear a traction engine, because that's what he meant. And I don't mind telling you another thing, and that is, Job was quite used to seeing his early potatoes cut off by the frost. That's what happened one morning when he went indoors and said the early spuds were finished, he meant those 'Which are black by reason of ice'.

Another thing I can tell you is this: if Job didn't live in the Fen, how did he know about the Denver Sluice? Yes, I thought that would make you open your eyes. Well, can anyone tell me what he meant if it wasn't the Denver Sluice he meant when he said: 'They have set doors and bars to keep out the sea.' And he knew, as well as you do, that doors didn't only keep out the sea but they kept the water in the river when it was needed. Haven't you stood on the river bank, just as a nice black frost was sealing the river in with a nice covering of ice, then, just before it was safe for skating, the men at the sluice opened the doors and let the water run out? And when you saw the ice fall in and go swirling down the Ten Mile, what did you say when you saw the finest bit of skating in the world spoilt? Now, don't look so sheepish; I know what words you used, as I did the same before I gave up swearing. Now, when Job saw the same thing happen, he didn't swear about the sluice-keeper. This is what he said: 'This is a heinous crime, yea it is an iniquity.' I agree with him there, and what's more, if the sluice had been opened like that in my father's time, they'd have murdered that keeper, and got away with it too.

There's another thing I can tell you. Job ground his pattens himself. Now, most of you have a little grindstone, haven't you? Well, who do you get to turn it when your pattens need grinding? Your wife, don't you? And so did Job, because that's why he said: 'Let the wife grind.' And not having any gloves on, her hands got cold and when she complained to Job about her chilblains, he said the same thing that you do: 'I

wash mine in snow.' And you all know that's the finest cure there is.

Most of you men here – and I've done the same thing myself – when you go to a skating match you like to buy a ticket in the sweepstake, don't you? Mind you, I'm not going so far as to prove it, but when he says, 'Every man shall draw after,' I take it he meant that, as he was running the sweep, he drew the first runner out of the hat and the others took their chance after. And there's something else I can tell you. You and I have seen some funny things when we've been skating, haven't we? I know I have. And when there are skaters there are laughs and a lot of sly winking going on. Now, you women, there's no need to go red in the face; I haven't said anything to make you do that. What I'm trying to make out to you is, that Job saw some funny things as well. Perhaps you'll be able to tell me, was it at a skating match, or somewhere else, that Job saw something that made him say: 'And what do my eyes wink at?'

Finally, brothers and sisters, I've done my best to prove to you there was ice and skaters thousands of years ago, and as I know most of you here have had other sporting times besides skating, I can tell you this: Job knew a lot more than he let out in his writings. I reckon, before the night's out, some of you will be making your way to where the long-tails sleep, to do the same that Job did: 'And abide in the covert to lie in wait.'

Well, I don't blame you. With this long black frost we're having, and so many being thrown out of work, most of you are hard put to it to know where the next meal's coming from. But I hope you won't lie too long in the coverts or you'll be late getting to Welney Washes tomorrow. I've been told, coming down here today, that there ought to be some fine skating, with plenty of good prize money. And though I'm standing in the chapel pulpit, I can tell you this: the parson at Welney, the Reverend Wilford, who's the best skater a man could ever want to see, is going to be the judge. And now,

before I close, I'd like to say that I've been telling you, today, what Job said. Now I'll tell you what I think myself about you all tomorrow: Good skating, I hope you win plenty of prize money, get home before dark, and keep off the beer.

In the Black Fens

LINDSAY WILLIAMSON

Skating aside, the Fens can be bone-chilling and bleak. Lindsay Williamson's poem evokes the windswept desolation of a Fenland winter.

The wind blows across the flat fens,
Reeds stir restlessly against each other,
The silence penetrates each and every furrow.

A heron glides effortlessly down into a dyke
in search of his meal.
He stands for a while, a grey and white
sentinel, daring a living thing to break
the peace.

As if by magic the scene changes to
one of wildness as billowing black
clouds emerge from the horizon.
Once proud elms now bare and dead

twist and turn as the stark fen betrays
their presence to the gale.

They stand, corpses, remnants of their
youth against the 'blow'.
Nothing but the saw will fell them.

The dykes and ditches begin to fill as the
black earth soaks then spits out the
moisture hurled on to it by the heavens.

The heron had no luck.
He drifts away from the drain as
silently as he came.

Eight Days Under
the Snow

HENRY GUNNING

*On a snowy day early in 1799, Elizabeth Woodcock, a
farmer's wife from the village of Impington, just north of
Cambridge, rode off to market as usual. By nightfall she
had not returned. In his* Reminiscences of the University, Town and County of Cambridge *Henry
Gunning tells her extraordinary story.*

· A Fenland Christmas ·

In the month of February of 1799 a very remarkable circumstance occurred of a woman being buried in a snow-drift eight days, and surviving the effects, although during the interval she had no other sustenance than that which the snow afforded.

It was the custom in those days for the wives of small farmers in the neighbourhood of Cambridge to come to market on horseback, bringing with them butter, fowls etc, and carrying home stores for the following week. On 2 February, Elizabeth Woodcock commenced her homeward journey to Impington (about two miles distant from Cambridge). Snow had fallen during the day, but she was not aware until she had proceeded about half the way how much it had drifted.

She managed to arrive within half a mile of her house, when she and her horse were startled by the appearance of a meteor. The horse immediately backed to the edge of a ditch, where its rider contrived to dismount, while the horse broke away, and proceeded to an open common. The woman followed in the vain hope he would return towards the main road.

Exhausted with the exertion, and benumbed with cold, she sat down upon the ground. At that time but little snow had drifted near her; but when she heard the clock of the village church strike eight, she was completely overwhelmed, and perfectly incapable, from her legs having become powerless, of making any exertion to extricate herself. When her horse returned home without her, a search was immediately commenced by the husband and some neighbours, which lasted for several days, in the course of which every snow-drift on her road home was diligently examined. To await the termination of the frost seemed the only alternative.

On the Sunday morning when it became daylight, she observed a small circular hole in the snow, and on the branch of a bush that was enclosed near her, she managed to fasten a coloured handkerchief, and to force it through the aperture, as

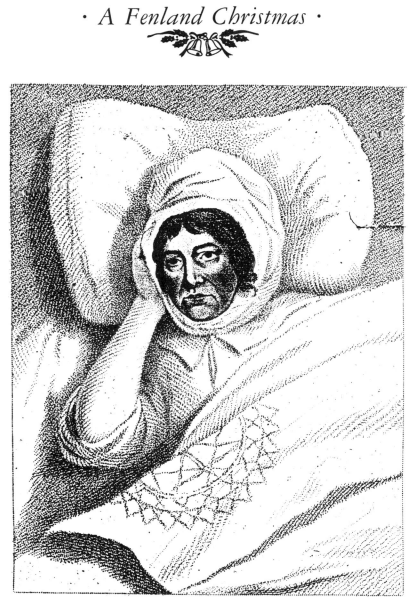

The unfortunate Elizabeth Woodcock

a signal of distress. But this expedient was of no avail until the following Sunday, when a young farmer passing over the common was attracted to the spot by the appearance of a flag. On removing it, and looking through the opening, he discovered the poor woman. Information was immediately given, and a cart procured to convey her home, where she had been for many days mourned by her husband and children as lost to them for ever.

She stated that during the period of her confinement she had slept but little; that she had never lost her consciousness; that she was perfectly sensible of the alternations of night and day; that she had distinctly heard the church-bells on the successive Sundays; that she had also heard carriages pass along the road; and had one day distinguished a conversation between some people, who she was sure were gipsies, but that they must have passed when her signal was not perceptible. She said that during the first night of her entombment she was much comforted by having been able to get at her snuff-box, but that on the following day she lost all sense of smelling. After she arrived home, a medical man was immediately sent for, but the reaction of the system produced so severe an illness that for some weeks she lingered between life and death.

As soon as she was considered sufficiently well to see company, persons thronged from all quarters, and there is little doubt that the consequent excitement shortened her life. She died the following July.

from
The Nine Tailors

DOROTHY L. SAYERS

*Brought up in Bluntisham-cum-Earith, where her father
was the local rector, Dorothy Sayers was no stranger to
harsh Fen winters. In this opening extract from* The Nine
Tailors, *one of her best-known mysteries, Lord Peter
Wimsey finds himself stuck in a snow-filled dyke as night
falls on New Year's Eve.*

'That's torn it!' said Lord Peter Wimsey.

The car lay, helpless and ridiculous, her nose deep in the
ditch, her back wheels cocked absurdly up on the bank, as
though she were doing her best to bolt to earth and were
scraping herself a burrow beneath the drifted snow. Peering
through a flurry of driving flakes, Wimsey saw how the
accident had come about. The narrow, hump-backed bridge,
blind as an eyeless beggar, spanned the dark drain at right
angles, dropping plumb down upon the narrow road that
crested the dyke. Coming a trifle too fast across the bridge,
blinded by the bitter easterly snowstorm, he had overshot the
road and plunged down the side of a dyke into the deep ditch
beyond, where the black spikes of a thorn hedge stood bleak
and unwelcoming in the glare of the headlights.

Right and left, before and behind, the fen lay shrouded. It

· A Fenland Christmas ·

A Boxing Day shoot near Wicken in the 1940s

was past four o' clock and New Year's Eve; the snow that had fallen all day gave back a glimmering greyness to a sky like lead.

'I'm sorry,' said Wimsey. 'Whereabouts do you suppose we've got to, Bunter?'

The manservant consulted a map in the ray of an electric torch.

'I think, my lord, we must have run off the proper road at Leamholt. Unless I am much mistaken, we must be near Fenchurch St Paul.'

As he spoke, the sound of a church clock, muffled by the snow, came borne upon the wind; it chimed the first quarter.

'Thank God!' said Wimsey. 'Where there is a church there is civilisation. We'll have to walk it. Never mind the suitcases; we can send somebody for them. Br'rh! It's cold. I bet that when Kingsley welcomed the wild northeaster he was sitting indoors by a good fire, eating muffins. I could do with a muffin myself. Next time I accept hospitality in the Fen-country, I'll take care that it's midsummer, or else I'll go by train. The church lies to windward of us, I fancy. It would.'

They wrapped their coats about them and turned their faces to the wind and snow. To the left of them, the drain ran straight as a rule could make it, black and sullen, with a steep bank shelving down to its slow, unforgiving waters. To their right was the broken line of a sunken hedge with, here and there, a group of poplars and willows. They tramped on in silence, the snow beating on their eyelids. At the end of a solitary mile the gaunt shape of a windmill loomed up upon the further bank of the drain, but no bridge led to it and no light showed.

Another half-mile and they came to a signpost and a secondary road that turned off to the right. Bunter turned his torch upon the signpost and read upon the single arm: 'Fenchurch St Paul.'

· *A Fenland Christmas* ·

Wicken Hall on a winter's day around 1910

There was no other direction; ahead, road and dyke marched
on side by side into the eternity of winter. 'Fenchurch St Paul
for us,' said Wimsey. He led the way into the side road, and as
he did so, they heard the clock again – nearer – chiming the
third quarter.

A few hundred yards of solitude, and they came upon the
first sign of life in this frozen desolation: on their left, the roofs
of a farm, standing some way back from the road, and, on the
right, a small, square building like a box of bricks, whose
sign, creaking in the blast, proclaimed it to be the Wheatsheaf
public-house. In front of it stood a small, shabby car, and from
windows on the ground and first floors light shone behind red
blinds.

Wimsey went up to it and tried the door. It was shut, but
not locked. He called out, 'Anybody about?' A middle-aged
woman emerged from an inner room.

'We're not open yet,' she began abruptly.

'I beg your pardon,' said Wimsey. 'Our car has come to grief. Can you direct us?'

'Oh, I'm sorry, sir. I thought you were some of the men. Your car broke down? That's bad. Come in. I'm afraid we're all in a muddle.'

'What's the trouble, Mrs Tebbutt?' The voice was gentle and scholarly, and, as Wimsey followed the woman into a small parlour, he saw that the speaker was an elderly parson.

Happy New Year, Cambridge!

In 1890 Cambridge people saw in the new year with sky rockets, while on New Year's Day loaves of bread and packets of tea were given away to the needy of the town. Here is the Cambridge Chronicle's *account of events.*

The advent of the new year was celebrated at Cambridge in the customary manner. Watchnight services were held and at midnight a large number of people gathered on the King's Parade to witness the display of sky rockets by Mr Deck. The weather was more 'seasonable' than that prevailing at Christmas, there being a slight covering of snow on the ground and a bright, keen atmosphere.

· A Fenland Christmas ·

On New Year's Day a very considerable commotion was caused in Barnwell by the novel distribution of Christmas gifts. The originator of the idea was Mr E. Sanderson, and the private appeal which was made for funds was very liberally responded to. Accordingly, a few days before the distribution, notices were posted that at twelve o'clock on Wednesday, 500 loaves of bread and 500 packets of tea would be given away at Mr Wallis's Saleroom on East Road, together with a glass of ale to all who chose to accept it.

To ensure order on the day it was arranged that the distribution should be by ticket, and for these there was a large demand, the distributors occasionally having a rough time of it. Outside the Saleroom a huge mainly female crowd gathered, swaying hither and thither, pushing, elbowing and squeezing to get to the front rank.

Inside the loaves of bread, all guaranteed to weigh 4 lb, were piled high upon a platform flanked by a portly 36 gallon cask of Armstrong's best ale. Mr Sanderson took up his station as distributor behind a small table in the centre of the room, with the packets of tea, each containing 2 ounces, by his side. When the signal was given that all was ready, there was a great rush, and the policeman on duty had considerable difficulty in avoiding being carried bodily away.

Notwithstanding this exhibition of eagerness, the crowd was a very orderly one and there was no attempt to force an entrance into the room. Those who declined the glass of ale were few indeed, and all who accepted it appeared to enjoy the refreshment after the struggle they had passed through. Perhaps the palm for age was taken by a hale and hearty old gentleman who claimed to be ninety-four though he looked quite twenty years younger.

Events of the Dying Year

GEORGE FLETCHER

As 1890 drew to a close, George Fletcher produced this lyrical 'review of the year' for the Cambridge Chronicle. *Then, as now, Russia and Ireland were in the news, as was football, 'the most dangerous game in the world'. Then, as now, Cambridge was growing fast, cyclists rode recklessly through the streets, roads needed repairing and accidents were common. The Victoria Bridge, however, then new, is crumbling now and having to be rebuilt. The other 'handsome and strong' bridge talked of as spanning the Cam at Abbey Road 'ere long', was not in fact opened until 1971!*

Farewell, old year, the time draws nigh,
When we must part, with tearful eye,
                              For ever.

Though brief thy life, as twill be seen
Full of events thy reign hath been,
                              Up to its close.

On our good Queen thou'st fondly smiled,
As doth a mother on her child,
                              God save the Queen.

135

· A Fenland Christmas ·

Those who would Monarchies destroy,
Find not that freedom we enjoy
                    In Republic nations.

With grief we daily hear the news
Of persecution of the Jews
                    In Holy Russia.

General Booth's Darkest England scheme
Deservedly hath won esteem
                    Of every class.

Though arts and science of every kind
Flow daily from the human mind,
                    'Twill flow more freely.

Yet education on every hand
Is in excess of the demand —
                    So scholars say.

Three score pianos the other day
Were ordered, so the papers say,
                    For London Board Schools.

Poor children now are over-crammed
With much they cannot understand,
                    Or like to need.

Hungry from school, no food at home,
Yearning for bread, starving they roam
                    About the streets.

With a plain and simple education
The English working population
                    Would be content.

· A Fenland Christmas ·

Stanley's travels are understood
To have done a vast amount of good.
>> I hope they have.

Yet if all facts were freely stated,
It might be found we've over-rated
>> His expedition.

Death and accidents, needless to name,
Prove football the most dangerous game
>> On earth.

Cyclists on all our roads are free,
Oft dangerous too; I fail to see
>> Why they're not taxed

Mr Balfour's done much to restore
Peace and comfort to the poor
>> Of Ireland.

Through recent scandal, it would seem
Home Rule hath vanished from the scene
>> Of practical politics.

In the land of shadows and romance,
An ill-conceived thing in a trance,
>> Home Rule's at rest.

Cambridge is growing day by day,
Improving, too, I'm bound to say,
>> In many ways.

Our University, the Nation's pride,
Now with the town works side by side,
>> For the good of both

· A Fenland Christmas ·

Of the Victoria Bridge, say what you will,
It's a piece of engineering skill
               Worthy of the town.

From the river side, the fact is plain,
Steps are required the bridge to gain.
               An item small.

Another bridge, handsome and strong,
Will span the Cam, I trust, ere long,
               Near Abbey Road.

The electric light and sewerage scheme,
Of which our local rulers dream,
               Are costly undertakings.

On the Val de Travers roads, I regret to say,
Accidents occur most every day –
               Is there no remedy?

Of Newmarket Road I must complain;
Lately repaired, yet after rain
               Observe the puddles.

Though years will come, and years will go,
May each New Year improvement show,
               For the public good.

I congratulate the worthy Mayor;
Impartially, he fills the chair
               As Chief Magistrate.

Ere on the old year falls the pall,
I wish, kind readers, one and all,
               A Bright New Year.

High Days and Holidays

SYBIL MARSHALL

Traditionally on Plough Monday, the first Monday after Twelfth Night, ploughmen in fanciful costumes decked with ribbons toured Fenland villages, dragging a decorated plough and collecting cash or cakes and ale from local villagers. In this second extract from Sybil Marshall's Fenland Chronicle, *Kate Mary Edwards recalls the fun to be had on Plough Monday when she was a child.*

Living where we did and how we did, we used to make the most of anything a bit out of the ordinary, and we looked for'ard from one special day to the next. Looking back on it now, I'm surprised to see how many high days and holidays there were during the year that we kept, and we certainly made the most of anything children could take part in.

Just after Christmas, there'd be Plough Witching to look for'ard to. This were Plough Monday, and of course I know that this is still kept in churches all over the land. But our Plough Monday ha'n't got nothing to do with churches as I knowed. There were two or three different things about it. For one thing there were the pranks the young fellows got up to, playing tricks on their neighbours. Very often these were real

· A Fenland Christmas ·

'Our Plough Monday ha'n't got nothing to do with churches as
I knowed.' Plough Monday boys in Swaffham Prior in 1929

nasty tricks, and they'd wait until Plough Monday to get their
own back on somebody what had done them some injury
during the year. Perhaps they'd take a plough in the middle of
the night and plough the other fellow's doorway up, or move
the water butt so as it stood resting on a bit of its bottom rim,
a-leaning up outside the door. Then when the man o' the
house opened the door afore it were light next morning, the
tub 'ould fall in and the water slosh all over the floor o' the
house-place, for the poor woman to clean up on her hands and
knees afore the children could come out o' the bedroom. Very
often a gang of young men 'ould go round the Fen taking gates
off their hinges and throwing 'em in the nearest dyke, so that
all the horses and cows got out. This sort o' nasty trick

gradually died out during my young days, and a good thing too I reckon.

Then there were the Straw Bear and the Molly Dancers. The Molly Dancers 'ould come round the Fen from Ramsey and Walton all dressed up. One would have a fiddle, and another a dulcimer, or perhaps a concertina and play while the rest danced. This were really special for Christmas Eve, but o' course the dancers couldn't be everywhere at once on one day, so they used to go about on any other special day to make up for it.

They'd go from pub to pub, and when they'd finished there, they'd go to any houses or cottages where they stood a chance o' getting anything. If we ha'n't got any money to give them, at least they never went away without getting a hot drink. Sometimes it 'ould be hot beer. In pubs they used to hot the beer by sticking a cone-shaped metal container down into the glowing turf fire, with the beer in it. Then it would be made syruppy sweet with brown sugar, and spiced with ginger, served with a long rod o' glass to break the sugar up and stir it with, for 2d a pint. At home it might be done in the same way, or it might simply have a red hot poker plunged into it. Sometimes the Molly Dancers got home-made elderberry wine, well-sugared and made scalding hot and spiced with cloves. A lot of the Fen women were very good at making wine, and their elderberry would be so dark and rich as you could hardly tell it from port wine. So a good tumbler full of that, all sweet and hot and spicy, were worth dancing for, and kept the cold out till they got to the next cottage.

The Straw Bear were a sort o' ceremony that took place on Plough Monday when I were a child, though my husband says it used to belong to some other day once and only got mixed up with Plough Witching time by chance. A party of men would choose one of their gang to be 'straw bear' and they'd start a-dressing him in the morning ready for their travels

Cromwell Morris Dancers celebrating Plough Monday in
Elsworth in 1990

round the Fen at night. They saved some o' the straightest,
cleanest and shiniest oat straw and bound it all over the man
until he seemed to be made of straw from head to foot, with
just his face showing. When night came they'd set out from
pub to pub and house to house, leading the straw bear on a
chain.

When they were asked in, the bear would go down on his
hands and knees and caper about and sing and so on. Some
parties used to do a play about 'Here I come I, old Beelzebub',
and there were another place where one man knocked another
one down, and then stood over him and said:

> Pains within and pains without
> If the devil's in, I'll fetch him out
> Rise up and fight again.

· A Fenland Christmas ·

I remember hearing about the year when Long Tom were the straw bear. His mates had spent the whole day from early morning getting him 'dorned out, and they were just about ready to start when he were took short and they had to pull all the straw off him quick to let him go to the closet. They weren't half savage with him, I can tell you, and they di'n't let him forget it for a goodish while.

What us children liked best were the Plough Witching, 'cos we could take part in that ourselves. We dressed up in anything we could find and blacked our faces with soot from the chimney to disguise ourselves. Then we went to our neighbours' houses and capered about on their doorways, or sang a song till they opened the door and let us in. There were a special song as we sung while we shook our collecting tin up and down:

> 'Ole in yer stocking
> 'Ole in yer shoe
> Please will yer give me a penny or two.
> If yew ain't got a penny
> A a'penny'll do,
> An' if yew ain't got an a'penny
> Well God bless yew!

Just one! Just one! Just one for the poor old ploughboy!
Just one! Just one! Just one!

This went on right up to the time my own children were little, and for all I know there's still some places where they don't let Plough Monday pass without somebody going a-Plough Witching, but I dessay folks are all too educated and clever to take pleasure in such simple things as that, nowadays.

The Straw Bear's Return

BRIAN KELL

*The Ramsey Straw Bear traditionally did the rounds of
the town on Plough Monday, while the Whittlesey Straw
Bear appeared the day after, on 'Straw Bear Tuesday'.
By the First World War, however, the custom in both
Fenland towns had largely died out. Then, in 1979,
folklore enthusiast Brian Kell, a newcomer to Whittlesey,
suggested a revival of the old tradition there. The Straw
Bear has 'danced' through the streets of Whittlesey on a
Saturday in early January ever since.*

A letter published in the Folk Lore Society's Journal in 1909
contains a description of Straw Bear Tuesday, which took place
in Whittlesey on the Tuesday following Plough Monday. The
Straw Bear was a man encased in straw who was 'danced' around
the town to entertain the locals and collect money. It seems the
Bear was frowned on by the local police and, to take the writer's
words, a primitive custom was suppressed by Bumbledom.

I first learnt about the Bear from a recorded narrative called
'Rattle Bone and Plough Jack'. It was not until I moved to
Whittlesey that I connected the two and, although a stranger
to the area, I had the audacity to make the following proposal
to the Whittlesey Society: 'I would like to revive The Straw

Bear and I am looking for the sanction of the people of Whittlesey to do so.'

What a reaction! The idea was received with great relish; other members of the society wondered why they had not thought of it before.

It was decided to dance the Straw Bear on the Saturday after Plough Monday so that more people could see it. The straw was provided by a local thatcher, Mr Dolby of Coates, and letters were sent to dance teams, Fenland District Council and the police.

The letter to the police was delivered by hand. The desk sergeant was moved to warn: 'Well, you know why it was stopped in the first place don't you.'

Nevertheless, the blessings of the authorities were received (despite the fact that the Law appeared to have an elephantine memory as well as a long arm), the dance teams accepted the invitation, and the day was set.

At 10.30 a.m. on Saturday 12 January 1980, a crowd of bemused onlookers and a large contingent from the press saw the Bear make its first appearance for many years. Assisted by Stevenage Sword and Northampton and Rutland Morris, the great beast shuffled from the town hall. A performance by the dancers in the market-place was followed by a walking tour of the town, visiting The Crown, The Ram, The Morton Fork, The New Crown, and The Black Bull, before returning to the market-place for a final dance after closing time. On went the strange gathering to St Mary's Parish Rooms where the dancers and Bear were fed and watered on soup, shepherd's pie and pints of tea.

After opening time, Stevenage Sword and the Bear moved on to the Bricklayer's Arms and The Letter B. At one time the imagination failed those responsible for naming pubs in Whittlesey so a lettering system was begun; The Letter A is now an art gallery. The troupe continued its progress to the Hero of Aliwal and on to The Boat, going back again to the parish rooms for an evening of song and dance. Singers were

provided by Peterborough and Stevenage Folk Clubs, a mummer's play performed by members of the Bretton Woods Country Dance Club, dance spots from Stevenage and Rutland, and tunes from a member of Fenland Morris. The small hall was crammed with Whittlesey people joining in the gusty songs. The final dance was performed by the Bear, at that stage in a tattered state.

Holding Court in the Guildhall

Revivals of old customs are not restricted to modern times. The 'Lord of Misrule' had his heyday in the fifteenth and sixteenth centuries, when he presided over revels lasting from All Hallow's Eve until Twelfth Night. In Cambridge in 1868 a somewhat sedate revival of this tradition was held in the Guildhall.

The Invitation

YE LORD OF MISRULE
WILL HOLD HIS
COURT IN THE GUILDHALL
ON THE EVENING OF
Thursday, January 2nd, 1868
In Holly Bower with Yule-Log and head of Boar
will he keep his Festival.

Before him will his lieges take their merry pastime, bells will they jingle, puppets will they play, carols will they sing, at the Quintain will they tilt; in wonder may they be dissolved.

To Shovel Board, to Fox and Goose, to view of life-whirling Cylinder, to Mother Goose, and to other ye games of ancientry and joyaunce does he invite his guests.

In the midst of his Court will rise a tree of marvellous fruit, from whose branches, in place of leaves, gauds and gems shall spring, the droppings whereof shall be transformed into work of cunning craftswomen.

To revive the energies of his liege-men and servants, the Lord of Misrule will provide drink from China, berries from Ceylon and flesh of pig.

The charge to prepare this Festival is given to the Wardens, Sidesmen and their fellows of the Parish of St Michael. A tribute of One Shilling current coin of the realm will be demanded. None will be allowed to enter the doors of the Hall who cannot produce a pass to certify that the tribute has been paid.

Whereas, moreover, the Christmas Tree of the Lord of Misrule produces wondrous fruits, he recommends that other coins be brought in the pocket, that exchanges may be effected, and memorials of the Yule festival of 1867 be preserved by his lieges.

The Festival will commence at six o'clock

The Event (as reported by the *Cambridge Chronicle*)

The Soirée and Christmas Festival announced by St Michael's parish took place in the Guildhall on Thursday evening. The entertainment was of a novel kind and thoroughly Christmas-like; there was a Christmas jollity on the platform; there was a Christmas air pervading the audience; there was a decidedly Christmas savour in the refreshment stall, and in the boar's

head which graced the table; even the dissolving views were on Christmas subjects.

With over six hundred people present, the entertainment was altogether a great success. From six o'clock till seven the audience promenaded to the strains of an excellent band provided by Mr Sippel, and in investing current coins of the realm at the Christmas tree and at the stall for the sale of an abundance of pretty and useful articles, eagerly pressed by the young ladies, who proved themselves such capital saleswomen, in fact, perfectly irresistible.

At seven, a procession of singers marched on the orchestra where had been erected a spacious bower for the reception of the Lord of Misrule. His lordship took his seat, with the hobbyhorse and dragon on either side, the lady singers, all similarly habited in Christmas costume, being on the right, the gentlemen on the left. His lordship delivered an appropriate prologue, inviting his guests to partake in the revels, and was followed by an exceedingly good selection of carols, very well sung. This, we might say, was the principal feature of the evening.

Then the spectators were invited to various games and to a Marionette Exhibition, but unfortunately, owing to the sudden indisposition of the young lady who was to have worked the puppets, the exhibition could not take place.

Another selection of music followed and a festive collection of dissolving views concluded the entertainment. We should mention that the Revd G. Weldon and the Senior Churchwarden of St Michael's gave two short readings which were, we fear, very indistinctly heard. Nevertheless, the whole affair was extremely well managed and reflected great credit on all concerned.

Cambridge Bellmen's Verses

Cambridge bellmen's verses are another more recent Christmas revival. The original bellmen shouted out advertisements and summonses by day, and called the hours through the night. At Christmas they gave out flysheets of verses and were generally rewarded with a tip in return. In 1984 Charles Hamilton revived the old tradition. These extracts give some flavour of bellmen's verses both ancient and modern.

Prologue

Ungenial Year! and shall thy gloom diffuse
Its misty terrors round your Bellman's muse –
Damp the strong impulse of poetic fire,
And chill the Christmas stanza on his lyre?
No! by Old Hobson – by the tuneful Nine,
If this should happen – 'tis no fault of mine.
At least permit it on your shelves to rise
In Christmas triumph round your cakes and pies.

Thomas Adams, Bellman, 1816

* * *

Prologue

Behold a stranger to the rhyming art,
Requests permission to perform his part;

From a Cambridge bellman's flysheet

And on his first appearance hopes to meet
Those cheering smiles which make his labours sweet.
Aware a poet he can never be,
He trusts to make it up by industry:
Give him your smiles; and tho' he writes not well,
By your approval he will bear the BELLE.

On Christmas Eve

Believe me, Maids, all things look very well;
Oh! what a charming and delicious smell
Is here of tarts and pies, by which I see
This surely will a merry Christmas be;
The spits adorn'd with roast beef, and such cheer,
The cellars full of ale and humming beer;
All things in order plac'd, and fitted too
For mirth and pastime, which will soon ensue.

Isaac Moule, Bellman, 1822

*   *   *

Prologue

Your Bellman, sirs, attempts again to greet
His worthy patrons with his annual sheet,
If times were brighter, light his verse would flow:
But they, like his lines are limping, sad and slow.
Those good old times are fled, when festive mirth
Join'd pious duties on the Saviour's birth;
Our ancestors, while they those feelings had,
With mirthful fantasies their hearts made glad;
And ever, as the Christmas Day drew near,
Prepar'd to treat their neighbours with good cheer.
Then would the great man open wide his door,
And all were welcom'd, whether rich or poor;

· A Fenland Christmas ·

The huge hall table then could boast,
Ample provision by the liberal host;
Round went the jest, the song, the merry tale,
Aided by wassail bowl and potent ale;
No nice distinction that day marked the board,
For all were equal – peasant, squire or lord.
Thus was the social compact every year maintained,
While kindest acts the aged poor sustained.
Your bard laments that times are so deranged
And good old customs so completely changed.
Sir Walter Scott doth his dissent proclaim
And in defence of them doth thus exclaim:
'England was merry England when
Old Christmas brought his sports again;
'Twas Christmas broached the mightiest ale;
'Twas Christmas told the merriest tale;
A Christmas gambol oft would cheer
A poor man's heart through half the year.'

                           Isaac Moule, Bellman, 1829

*   *   *

Prologue

O worthy sirs, I hope you'll think it meet
To resurrect the Cambridge Bellman's Sheet.
A duty first discharged by Samuel Saul –
In 1757 he received the call:
For thirty years he served the city well
Till Thomas Adams rang the famous Bell.
Then 1820 dawned and in the role
A Bellman new – the junior Isaac Moule.
Continued he till 1854;
And then alas – our Bellman was no more.
So now we come unto the present year,

152

And Orwell's doleful dream draws ever near –
But may my predecessors guide me well
To serve with honour Cantab's famous Bell.
You'll not deny we live in parlous times –
And who can cheer if not a man of rhymes?
Therefore good sirs – I pray – 'tis my intent
To make this sheet an annual event
Restoring proud tradition is my aim;
The Bellman lives – who reads me will exclaim!

On Christmas Day

'The bells of waiting Advent ring'
Then happy shouts of children sing.
Glad tidings now to all we bring –
On Christmas Day.
And gifts beneath the Christmas tree
Are brought and giv'n lovingly
To such as you, and such as me –
On Christmas Day.
But let us ever yet recall,
The greatest gift to man of all
Was born into a lowly stall –
On Christmas Day.
So may we all then humbler be,
Live out our lives accordingly;
Resolving to be more like he –
On Christmas Day.

To The Grafton Centre

Let cymbals sound; let trumpets bray;
From Debenhams to C & A!
The Grafton Centre's open doors
Shew vaulted roof o'er marble floors.

· A Fenland Christmas ·

O many are the wonders there,
Aladdin's cave would scarce compare!
Exotic tree-lined shopping mall,
And scenic lifts atop it all.
But will it suit old Cam' you say?
Well, only time will show the way;
For hearken to the Lion Yard
That left our city centre scarr'd –
But come – let us not churlish be,
Instead good will, prosperity –
To all your trades, both great and small;
The town bidd'st welcome to you all!

Epilogue

Your humble servant, sirs, I now remain;
Yet hope to be of service once again.
May Heav'n's blessings come unto your door –
And save us all – in 1984.

Charles Hamilton, Bellman, 1984

Blue Caps and Red Cloaks

Near, rather than in, the Fens, Sandringham was bought by Queen Victoria for the Prince of Wales (later Edward VII) in 1861. By 1866, this local newspaper report suggests, Christmas charity on the estate had become a highly-organized affair.

Yesterday, Christmas Day, the good old custom of making presents which has been established during his Royal Highness's ownership of the estate was observed. In the morning the children of the schools were marched up to Park House where they received their annual gifts of clothing. Each boy was presented with a tweed jacket and a blue cap, and each girl with a red cloak and a hat.

At four o'clock in the afternoon all the cottagers, labourers, carpenters, bricklayers, gardeners etc. employed on the estate, residing in the parishes of Sandringham, Babingley, West Newton, Wolferton and Dersingham, assembled in the park, near the royal stables, the centre of attraction being the coach house, round the sides of which were ranged tables groaning under the weight of sixty two stones nine pounds of the primest joints of beef, all cut up and ticketed, and ranged according to parishes.

Soon after four o'clock the royal party returned from an excellent day's shooting at Houghton, and the Prince of Wales and the Duke of Edinburgh entered the carriage house which was tastefully decorated with evergreens, and immediately after the presentation commenced.

The beef was distributed according to number in the family, in the proportion of 2 lb each for the man and woman and 1lb each for the children. Each widow received 4 lb of beef. The total number of families receiving meat was 169, representing 616 people. Mr Beck, agent, and Mr Carmichael, head gardener, handed over the beef to the recipients one by one as they were called by name, each paying his obeisance to his Royal Highness. This morning the Sandringham choristers marched from the schoolhouse to the terrace about one o'clock and sang some pretty Christmas anthems.

The Prince and Princess of Wales and the Duke of Edinburgh were present at divine service in the pretty little church in the park. This afternoon all the schoolchildren, in their new cloaks and jackets, were marched up to Sandringham House to pay their obeisance to the royal family. The passing by was witnessed by the Prince and Princess of Wales, Princes Albert, Victor and George, and the Duke of Edinburgh. Each child received a Christmas bun, and then dispersed to their homes.

Night falls on a Fenland winter's day

Acknowledgements

I should like to thank Mike Petty and staff of the Cambridgeshire Collection for all their patience and invaluable help.

'Hetty Pegler's Christmas' by Celia Dale is reprinted from *Cambridgeshire & Peterborough Life*, December 1974, by permission of *Cambridgeshire & Peterborough Life* and the author; 'Christmas Memories', from *Reflections of a Country Woman* by Mabel Demaine, Haddenham, 1989, by permission of Mrs Lorna Delanoy; 'Old Christmas', from *Wisbech Standard*, 20 December 1889; 'Memories of a Soham Butcher', from *Life in the Meat Trade* by Ken Isaacson, Soham Books, 1989, by permission of the author; 'Christmas Dinners that Walked to London', from *A Tour Through The Whole Island of Great Britain* by Daniel Defoe, 1724; 'In Memory of a Turkey', from *Ely Standard*, 26 December 1913; 'Wisbech Christmas Show', from *Wisbech Standard*, 20 December 1895; 'Christmas Treats' by Blanche Looker as told to Michael Rouse, from *Cambridgeshire & Peterborough Life*, December 1976, by permission of *Cambridgeshire & Peterborough Life* and Michael Rouse; 'Christmas Advertising, Victorian Style', from *Cambridge Chronicle*, 19 December 1868, and *Wisbech Standard*, 19 December 1890 and 25 December 1891; 'Seasonable Suggestions', from *Wisbech Standard*, 25 December 1896; 'Saving Time on Christmas Shopping', from *Cambridgeshire & Peterborough Life*, December 1967, with their permission; 'Peterborough Cathedral's Silent Christmas Bells' by Trevor A. Bevis, from *Cambridgeshire & Peterborough Life*, December 1972, by permission of *Cambridgeshire & Peterborough Life* and the author; 'Cambridge to Ely by Mail Coach' was written by Chris Carling; 'The Festival of Carols at King's College' by Irene Lister, from *Cambridgeshire & Peterborough Life*, December 1971, by permission of *Cambridgeshire & Peterborough Life* with acknowledgement to the author; 'Larking and Practical Joking', from *Memoirs of a King's College Chorister* by Thomas H. Case, 1899; 'Sing All Ye Merry' by Jack Overhill, from *East Anglian Magazine*, December 1974, by permission of Jack Overhill Jn.; 'Good King Wenceslas' by William Abington, from *Cambridgeshire & Peterborough Life*, December 1980, by permission of *Cambridgeshire & Peterborough Life* with acknowledgement to the author; 'A Christmas Eve Wedding' and 'High Days and Holidays', from *Fenland Chronicle* by Sybil Marshall, Cambridge University Press, 1967, by permission of Cambridge University Press and the author; 'Hereward's Return', from *The Camp of Refuge, A Tale of the Conquest of the Isle of Ely* by Charles Macfarlane, with notes by S.H. Miller, Simpkin, Marshall & Co., 1878 (first published anonymously in 1844); an extract from 'Hymn on the Morning of Christ's Nativity' by John Milton, 1629; 'Dad's Christmas' by Lindsay Williamson, by permission of the author; 'A Victorian Christmas' by John Durrant, from *Cambridgeshire & Peterborough Life*, December 1983, by permission of *Cambridgeshire & Peterborough Life* and the author; 'Ode by a Christmas Pudding at Sea' by Arthur Locker, from *Cambridge Chronicle*, 26 December 1890; '"Welcome to the Poor of Walsoken"', from *Wisbech Standard*, 3 January 1890; 'A Sober Christmas in King's Lynn', from *Cambridge Chronicle*, 9

January 1841; 'College Feasting' and 'An Icy Road to Ely', from *The Cantab, or A Few Adventures and Misadventures in After Life* by the Revd H.I.C. Blake, 1845; 'Skating on Whittlesey Mere', from *Cambridge Chronicle*, 2 January 1841; 'The Fen Skaters of Welney Wash' by Frances Collingwood, from *East Anglian Magazine*, January 1950, with acknowledgement to the author; 'The Duddleston Cup' by C. Woode, 1895, from *The Skaters of the Fens* by Alan Bloom, W. Heffer and Sons, 1958, by permission of Alan Bloom; 'A Sermon on Skating', from *Tales of the Fens* by W.H. Barrett, edited by Enid Porter, Routledge and Kegan Paul, 1963, by permission of the publishers; 'In the Black Fens', from *Fen Folk* by Lindsay Williamson, Spiegl Press, 1987, by permission of the author; 'Eight Days Under the Snow', from *Reminiscences of the University, Town and County of Cambridge from the year 1780*, volume 2, by Henry Gunning, 1854; an extract from *The Nine Tailors* by Dorothy L. Sayers, Victor Gollancz, 1934, by permission of David Higham Associates; 'Happy New Year, Cambridge!', from *Cambridge Chronicle*, 3 January 1890; 'Events of the Dying Year' by George Fletcher, from *Cambridge Chronicle*, 26 December 1890; 'The Straw Bear's Return' (first published as 'How the Whittlesey Straw Bear Found his Way Back to Town') by Brian Kell, from *Cambridgeshire & Peterborough Life*, April 1983, by permission of *Cambridgeshire & Peterborough Life* and the author; 'Holding Court in the Guildhall', from *Cambridge Chronicle*, 4 January 1868; Cambridge Bellman's verses, 1984, by Charles Hamilton, by permission of the author; 'Blue Caps and Red Cloaks', from *Cambridge Chronicle*, 29 December 1868.

Picture Credits

Cambridge and County Folk Museum, pp. 44, 140; *Cambridge Evening News*, pp. 7, 142; Cambridgeshire Collection, pp. 10, 34, 59, 63, 66, 69, 86, 90, 102, 104, 107, 109, 112, 117, 127, 150, 156; Cambridgeshire Collection, from *Hereward the Brave*, by Julia Corner, 1870, pp. 78, 81; Anthony Day Collection, pp. 11, 74, 121, 130, 132; Chris Carling, pp. 53, 54; Margaret George Collection, Brian Payne, p. 32; Dorothy Grainger Collection, Cambridgeshire Collection, p. 21; Charles Harper, from *The Cambridge, Ely and King's Lynn Road*, 1902, p. 99; Brian Human, pp. 2, 5, 45, 46; King's College, Cambridge, p. 61; Mr and Mrs Derek Leonard, p. 18; Lilian Ream Collection, Cambridgeshire Libraries, pp. 27, 29, 41; Michael Rouse, p. 17; the illustration of Sandringham Church on the title page is reproduced from *Sunrise-Land, Rambles in Eastern England* by Annie Berlyn, 1894.